Ten Tales for Teaching English

**Stories and Activities for Children
Acquiring English**

by

Ellen M. Balla

Good Year Books

An Imprint of Pearson Learning

Good Year Books

are available for most basic curriculum subjects plus many enrichment areas. For more Good Year Books, contact your local bookseller or educational dealer. For a complete catalog with information about other Good Year Books, please write:

Good Year Books
299 Jefferson Road
Parsippany, NJ 07054

Book Design: Street Level Studio
Illustrations: Street Level Studio

Copyeditor: Rebecca Rauf
Production Editor: Laura Alavosus

Editorial Manager: Suzanne Beason
Executive Editor: Judith Adams
Publisher: Rosemary Calicchio

I SBN 0-673-59240-5

1 2 3 4 5 6 7 8 9 – ML – 06 05 04 03 02 01 00

Table of Contents

Fairy tales provide a fun and exciting way to introduce children to the world of literature. Children enjoy hearing, reading, and acting out tall tales, and they have fun participating in activities that complement these stories. When stories are presented in an enjoyable manner, children's interest is sparked and they develop a hunger for more stories and literature.

Ten Tales for Teaching English opens a door that allows children to develop their interest in literature as they explore and learn the English language. Ten familiar stories from many cultures are accompanied by activities that focus on vocabulary, grammar, and communication objectives. The stories have been selected for their high interest level, and are engagingly presented in rhyming couplets that preserve the natural flow of the story and language. The language level, content, and activities are appropriate for children in grades K–2 who are beginning or intermediate students of English as a second language.

Some children will have learned these stories in their native languages. This will be an advantage for them when the story is presented, as they will be able to draw on their prior knowledge. In addition, the stories offer children a chance to share aspects of their native cultures and learn about other cultures, thus fostering a community atmosphere in the classroom.

Ten Tales for Teaching English is designed to supplement any beginning or intermediate ESL curriculum. The stories and activities focus on vocabulary, grammar structures, communication skills, learning strategies, and thinking skills commonly taught in classrooms and basal series at this level. The activities encompassing these skills are challenging, fun, and relevant. They achieve the objectives through a hands-on approach that encourages children to speak as much English as possible. Many activities involve working in pairs or groups to facilitate the goal of students working and cooperating with their peers. As much content area as possible is included to help keep ESL students current in the mainstream content areas and to support the mainstream classroom efforts.

These units can be used in a variety of ways to complement your existing curriculum. They are particularly useful as an exciting and challenging review of vocabulary and grammar taught in other contexts. Each unit of the book addresses all four language skills: listening, speaking, reading, and writing. You may use any or all of the activities accompanying a story, depending on the interests and abilities of your students and the constraints of your schedule, classroom, and curriculum. Students who have acquired more English can be challenged to work on a higher level. Give them a copy of the story and have them read silently as you read the story to them. Encourage them to write about the story in their own words and to share their work with the rest of the class. Other suggestions for more advanced learners are included in the Additional Activities section of each unit.

Teachers who are attempting to "totally immerse" their children in English will particularly enjoy this book. By incorporating so many aspects of language and literature, *Ten Tales for Teaching English* can help ESL children reach their goals in the target language sooner.

Each unit includes a set of **teacher preparation pages** to help direct the learning around the story. These pages provide

- a synopsis of the story

- a list of the literature, grammar, communication, and content-area objectives for the unit

- a warm-up activity to help students focus on the upcoming story

- a list of important vocabulary and grammatical structures from the story

- suggestions for teaching and reviewing the unit vocabulary and grammar, including model conversations for students to practice

- directions for using the student pages

- additional activities

The **student pages** in each unit begin with the story (divided into two parts with comprehension questions) and include practice, application, and evaluation pages. The story and activity pages are intended to be photocopied and distributed to students.

Other features of the book include

- **Scope and Sequence of Skills:** This essential reference section lists the specific objectives for each unit.

- **Presenting the Story Units:** This section contains general guidelines and suggestions for planning and presenting a story unit.

- **Flashcards:** These reproducible pages provide illustrations of key vocabulary words and concepts from the stories. A flashcard is included for each starred word in the unit vocabulary lists. Suggestions for using the flashcards are included in the teacher preparation pages for each unit and in Presenting the Story Units. In addition, pages 169–170 contain instructions for seven games that students can play with the flashcards.

- **Suggestions for Additional Reading:** This bibliography offers a list of additional reading material and sources for other versions of the fairy tales in this book.

3

The Three Bears

Grammar Objectives
Simple present tense of regular verbs and verb *to be*; predicate adjectives; answer *who/what/how* questions in the simple present; singular and plural nouns

Communication Objectives
Make introductions; talk about how one feels; make apologies

Learning Strategies and Thinking Skills
Understand sequence; use illustrations; follow directions; use rhyme; cooperate with peers; use prior knowledge; make predictions; self-assess

Content Connection
Language arts; literature; math — counting and number recognition

Cinderella

Grammar Objectives
Simple present tense of regular verbs and verb *to be*; predicate adjectives; answer *who/what/how* questions in the simple present; preposition *at* with expressions of time

Communication Objectives
To talk about time; to tell time

Learning Strategies and Thinking Skills
Understand sequence; use illustrations; follow directions; use rhyme; use prior knowledge; cooperate with peers; make predictions; self-assess

Content Connection
Language arts; literature; math — counting and number recognition

The Little Red Hen

Grammar Objectives
Simple present tense of regular verbs and verb *to be*; use *will* to make a request or promise; use *won't* to refuse to do something; answer *who/what/how* questions in the simple present

Communication Objectives
To make requests; to make promises; to refuse to do something; to talk about how plants grow; to talk about and identify animals

Learning Strategies and Thinking Skills
Understand sequence; understand process of events; use illustrations; follow directions; understand cause and effect; use rhyme; relate story to real life; use prior knowledge; cooperate with peers; make predictions; self-assess

Content Connection
Language arts; literature; science

Catch the Bun

Grammar Objectives	Simple present tense of regular verbs and verb *to be*; predicate adjectives; answer *who/what/how* questions in the simple present; modal *can*
Communication Objectives	To talk about animals; to talk about baby animals and their mothers
Learning Strategies and Thinking Skills	Understand sequence; use illustrations; classify; follow directions; use rhyme; use prior knowledge; cooperate with peers; make predictions; self-assess
Content Connection	Language arts; literature; science

The Hungry Goat

Grammar Objectives	Simple present tense of regular verbs and verb *to be*; predicate adjectives; answer *who/what/how* questions in the simple present; commands
Communication Objectives	To talk about animals; to talk about the different sounds that animals make; to sing a song in English; to talk about how one feels
Learning Strategies and Thinking Skills	Understand sequence; use illustrations; follow directions; use rhyme and music; use prior knowledge; cooperate with peers; relate to real life; make predictions; self-assess
Content Connection	Language arts; literature; music

The Three Billy Goats

Grammar Objectives	Simple present tense of regular verbs and verb *to be*; adjectives; commands; answer *who/what/how* questions in the simple present; use prepositions; use the intensifier *very*
Communication Objectives	To talk about the size of things; to talk about where things are; to describe objects
Learning Strategies and Thinking Skills	Understand sequence; use illustrations; classify; follow directions; compare and contrast; use rhyme; listen for details; use prior knowledge; cooperate with peers; make predictions; self-assess
Content Connection	Language arts; literature; math; art

Anansi and the Eggs

Grammar Objectives	Simple present tense of regular verbs and verb *to be*; predicate adjectives; answer *who/what/how* questions in the simple present; possessive adjectives; singular and plural nouns; count nouns
Communication Objectives	To count from 1–8; to talk about how many objects there are; to talk about possession of objects; to talk about and identify animals
Learning Strategies and Thinking Skills	Understand sequence; use illustrations; classify; follow directions; use rhyme; listen for details; use prior knowledge; cooperate with peers; make predictions; self-assess
Content Connection	Language arts; literature; math

The Stonecutter

Grammer Objectives	Simple present tense of regular verbs and verb *to be*; predicate adjectives; comparative adjectives; answer *who/what/how* questions in the simple present
Communication Objectives	To talk about wishes; to talk about the weather
Learning Strategies and Thinking Skills	Understand sequence; use illustrations; follow directions; compare and contrast; use rhyme; relate to real life; listen for details; use prior knowledge; cooperate with peers; identify with character; make predictions; self-assess
Content Connection	Language arts; literature; science; art

The Wishes

Grammar Objectives	Simple present tense of regular verbs and verb *to be*; predicate adjectives; answer *who/what/how* questions in the simple present; singular and plural nouns; mass nouns
Communication Objectives	To talk about different kinds of food; to tell what one wants to eat; to tell what one has; to talk about wishes
Learning Strategies and Thinking Skills	Understand sequence; use illustrations; follow directions; use rhyme; use prior knowledge; make wishes; relate to real life; cooperate with peers; make predictions; self-assess
Content Connection	Language arts; literature; science — nutrition

Ten Tales for Teaching English © Good Year Books.

Paul Bunyon

Grammar Objectives
Simple present tense of regular verbs and verb *to be*; adjectives; answer *who/what/how* questions in the simple present; similes; singular and plural nouns

Communication Objectives
To describe things and people using similes; to talk about legends and reality; to talk about body parts; to talk about the United States; to talk about where one lives and where one is from

Learning Strategies and Thinking Skills
Understand sequence; use illustrations; follow directions; compare and contrast; use rhyme; identify with character; identify realism and fantasy; relate part to whole; use prior knowledge; make connection with real life; cooperate with peers; make predictions; self-assess

Content Connection
Language arts; literature; social studies; science

The story units are designed to be presented in more than one session so children will not be overloaded with new material. This section contains guidelines for presenting a story unit in six 30-minute lessons. As you become familiar with these guidelines, you may want to adapt them to suit the specific needs of your students and your learning environment. To assist in this adaptation, photocopy and complete a Unit Planning Guide for each story unit (see page 17). The Unit Planning Guide will help you decide which material to review and which material to present as new.

Lesson One

Your first lesson should begin with a warm-up activity that sparks students' interest in the story, focuses their attention on the story topic, and allows students to draw on past experiences and prior knowledge. For example, show pictures and ask students to tell what they know about any animals, special objects, or places that are part of the story. Give the story title and invite students to share anything they already know about the story—perhaps by drawing a picture.

Help students understand that they will be reading this story and completing activities about it. Specific suggestions for warm-up activities appear in the teacher preparation pages for each story unit.

Next, preview the vocabulary and grammar included in the unit. Once you have determined which words and structures your students will need to work on, choose from the following activities:

Verbs

Begin by showing children any appropriate flashcards or other visual aids for the verbs. (Flashcards for starred words in the vocabulary lists are printed on pages 156–164 at the end of this book.) Have students work with the simple present tense. Monitor their pronunciation of the final *s* as /s/ and /z/. Act out the verbs for students and have them take turns acting out the verbs for each other. Model the new words and have students repeat them after you as a group and then individually so you can check for individual pronunciation.

Ten Tales for Teaching English © Good Year Books.

If students need additional activities to reinforce the final sounds /s/ and /z/, use the following minimal pair exercises. Have children listen to the pairs of words first. After they can hear the difference between the two words, have them practice saying the pairs.

Teacher: *I am going to say two words. Please tell me if they are the same or different.*

                knees   knees

Students: *same*

Teacher: *knees   niece*

Students: *different*

Teacher: *I am going to say two words. Listen carefully and then say them.*

                knees   knees

Students: *knees   knees*

Teacher: *knees   niece*

Students: *knees   niece*

Below are some other minimal pairs you can use.

peace	peas
bus	buzz
place	plays
pace	pays
race	rays
trace	trays
fleece	fleas
ice	eyes
price	prize
rice	rise
fuss	fuzz

The stories are all written in the simple present tense. Lessons Two and Three suggest activities you can use if your students are ready for additional verb tense work.

Nouns

When presenting the nouns for the story, use the flashcards and any other appropriate visual aids or realia. Present the singular noun forms first, then the plurals. Monitor students' pronunciation, making sure they pronounce each final *s* with the correct /s/ or /z/ sound. If your students need more practice hearing and saying these final sounds, use the minimal pair activities described in the Verbs section.

Check for comprehension by showing a visual aid and asking children to tell you what you are holding up. Encourage students to answer using complete sentences and to draw on past experience and prior knowledge when possible. If realia are available, play the "What is it?" game. Put the realia in a bag and have children take turns choosing an item with their eyes closed. Ask, "What is it?" Have students try to guess what they are holding.

If your students need more work with singular and plural nouns, use the following activity:

Change it!
Hold up a visual aid for a singular noun and have students identify it. Tell them that they are going to change the word to show more than one. Model the following for them:

Teacher: *bear*   *bears*
               chair   *chairs*

Write the words on the chalkboard and label the columns *One* and *More Than One*. Help children notice that the plural words have an *s* at the end. Ask students to give other singular nouns and then to add *s* to make them plural. Write them on the chalkboard in the correct columns.

More advanced students can say complete sentences. Use the following model as a guide.

Ten Tales for Teaching English © Good Year Books.

Teacher: *(holding up a picture of a bear) It is a bear.*
They are bears.

You may wish to introduce the contractions *it's* and *they're*. If so, write the complete form and the contracted form on the chalkboard and help students see that some letters in the words have been taken out and replaced with an apostrophe in the contraction.

Adjectives

Introduce or review the adjectives from the story by using visual aids or by acting out the words. After students are familiar with the new vocabulary, play charades. Have children take turns acting out an adjective from the story. The first student to correctly guess a word gets to act out the next word.

To check students' comprehension of the story vocabulary, use a drawing dictation. Give each student a piece of drawing paper and demonstrate how to fold it into a certain number of boxes (anywhere from four to sixteen) and then open it up again. Dictate that number of vocabulary words and have students illustrate each one. When they are finished, they can share their work with a partner or the class.

For additional practice with the story grammar and vocabulary, use the model conversation(s) provided in the teacher preparation pages for each story unit. Model a conversation for students. After they are familiar with it, have them repeat it after you. Let pairs of students practice it. Then have children switch parts and act out the conversation. As a closing activity, ask students to change the conversation, following the grammar pattern but substituting other vocabulary words. Model if necessary.

Lesson Two

Use the story illustrations, flashcards, and any additional visual aids to review the story topic, vocabulary, and grammar presented in Lesson One. Encourage students to talk about the illustrations and what the story will be about. Then read Part 1 of the story to them. For students who are already reading in English, provide a copy of the story and have them read silently as you read aloud. Ask the questions at the bottom of the page to check for comprehension.

Read Part 1 of the story again. Then ask students to say a sentence that tells something that happened in Part 1. Model a sentence for them, such as *The bears go to the park.* Note that the stories are all written in the simple present tense. If your students are ready for additional verb tense work, try using the simple past tense for this activity. *(The bears went to the park.)*

As students contribute their sentences, write them on the chalkboard. Then help students read the sentences and sequence them to reflect the order of events in the story. Students who are not yet reading in English can do this activity if you read the sentences aloud as needed during the sequencing.

Students who are familiar with the future tense can talk about what they think is going to happen next. Have them draw or write their predictions and save them for the next lesson. After you have read Part 2 of the story, have children compare the story ending with their predictions.

For a simpler closing activity, have children draw pictures of the events and characters in Part 1 and share their work with a partner or the class.

Lesson Three

Use the story illustrations, flashcards, and any additional visual aids to review Part 1 of the story. Focus students' attention on any illustrations that show what is going to happen in Part 2 of the story. If students have made story predictions, review their work and talk about what they think is going to happen in Part 2. Elicit as much new vocabulary as possible and draw on children's prior knowledge and experiences.

Read Part 2 of the story aloud. If appropriate, distribute copies of Part 2 for children to follow along silently as you read aloud. Ask the questions at the bottom of the page to check for comprehension.

Ten Tales for Teaching English © Good Year Books.

Read the story again and then ask children a question such as "What do the bears do?" or "What does Goldilocks do?" Model a statement that answers the question, using the simple present tense (e.g., "The bears come back."). Ask students to tell other things that the characters do, using simple present tense verbs. Use the flashcards, the story illustrations, or any additional visual aids to help students focus on the activity.

As students contribute their sentences, write them on the chalkboard under the heading *Happens All the Time*. When everyone has had a turn, help students read their sentences. Make a new column and label it *Happened Already, Happening Now,* or *Going to Happen.* Have students change their sentences to fit the verb tense you have chosen. Write the revised sentences in the new column.

As a closing activity, have students draw a picture of their favorite character from the story. Let them share their work with the class and tell why they like this character the best. Children who are already reading and writing in English can write one or two sentences about why this is their favorite character.

A more advanced closing activity is to read sections from the story, leaving out key words for the students to fill in. First write a word list on the chalkboard and help students read the words with you. Place illustrations or realia next to the words for students who are not yet reading in English. Use the following as a model:

chair	Goldilocks	hot	park

Teacher:	*Goldilocks sits in Father's big _____.*
Students:	*chair*

Teacher:	*Father goes to the bedroom and sees _____.*
Students:	*Goldilocks*

Ten Tales for Teaching English © Good Year Books.

| Teacher: | *The bears' food is too _____.* |
| Students: | *hot* |

| Teacher: | *The bears go to the _____.* |
| Students: | *park* |

Lesson Four

This lesson uses the practice page to review and reinforce the story, characters, and vocabulary. Use the flashcards, story illustrations, and any other visual aids to preview the material on the practice page. After children are familiar with the necessary vocabulary, grammar structures, and topics, show them a copy of the practice page. Have them talk about the pictures and the activity they will be doing. The practice pages include a variety of hands-on games, puzzles, and other activities.

Model how the page is to be completed. Then hand out copies of the practice page for students to complete in pairs. Refer to the teacher preparation pages in each story unit for specific practice page guidelines and suggestions for activities to close Lesson Four.

Lesson Five

This lesson focuses on the application page. These pages provide a bridge between the ESL curriculum and the mainstream curriculum, using vocabulary, grammar, and topics that relate to content areas such as math, social studies, health, music, and science. Each page contains a story, poem, finger play, activity, or song that incorporates additional vocabulary related to a specific content area.

Begin the lesson with a warm-up activity that encourages students to tell what they already know about the application page topic. Then follow the suggestions in the teacher preparation pages for each unit and use one of the additional activities as a closing activity.

Lesson Six

This lesson focuses on the evaluation page, which is designed to check students' comprehension of the story, vocabulary, and grammar objectives for the unit. Begin with a warm-up that allows students to review the characters and what happened in the story. Focus students' attention on the topic for this page and use the story illustrations, flashcards, or any additional realia that will help students draw on their past experiences. Encourage them to use complete sentences in the target verb tense and as much of the vocabulary from this unit as possible. Next, tell students what activity they will be doing and model how the evaluation page is to be completed. Give each student a copy of the page to complete independently.

Have students work in groups to act out the story using the story dialogue. Students who have acquired more English can put the story into their own words or write their own dialogues. As an alternative activity, have students tell who their favorite characters are and why.

To close the unit, ask students to complete the Now I Know page (see page 18). Write *Now I Know* on the chalkboard and ask students to share details about the story. Draw or write key words as children discuss what happened. Next, tell children that they are going to either draw or write about what happened in the story. Give each student a copy of the Now I Know page, and model how to complete it. Students can draw about some aspect of the story or illustrate key vocabulary words they have learned. The lines at the bottom of the page are provided for students who have acquired more English. Have these students write about their drawings and about what they have learned in the story unit.

Additional activities are provided in each story unit so you can create lessons that best suit the needs of your students. Use these activities as warm-ups, closing activities, or for additional practice in an area that you need to reinforce. Begin each activity by showing students visual aids that relate to the topic. Have them talk about what they see. Next, tell them what activity they will be doing and model how the activity is done. After students have completed the activity, have them talk about it and, if possible, tell how it relates to the story.

Students who have acquired more English will enjoy the writing exercises that focus on the story, vocabulary, comprehension, and a specific reading skill—usually rhyming words. Again, do a warm-up with children as described above and explain what the activity entails. Have students complete the activity with a partner, and then share their work with the class.

The evaluation page of the story "Paul Bunyon" is a "bingo" board that can be used with any of the stories in a few different ways (see page 154). If possible, make enlarged copies of the board for each student. Then, make reduced copies of the appropriate flashcards found at the back of the book and have students paste them in a random order on their bingo boards. Provide students with markers, such as paper clips, and play bingo in the usual way.

Students who have acquired more English can play a more challenging game. Review the vocabulary for the bingo game using the corresponding visual aids/realia and write the words on the board. Have students copy the words, in a random order, in the spaces on their bingo boards. Then, either read or show the visual aid for the word and have students play bingo in the usual way.

Ten Tales for Teaching English © Good Year Books.

Unit Planning Guide

Story: _____ Date: _____

Class: _____

Words that Children Already Know

Words that I Need to Teach

Grammar/Lexical Frames that Children Already Know

Grammar/Lexical Frames that I Need to Teach

Now I Know

Name: _____

Story: _____

Draw or write about the story.

_____
_____
_____
_____
_____
_____

OverView

Story Synopsis

Three bears—Mama Bear, Papa Bear, and Baby Bear—sit down to eat their food and find that it is too hot. They decide to take a walk. While they are taking a walk, a girl named Goldilocks enters the house. She eats their food, sits in their chairs, breaks Baby Bear's chair, and then takes a nap in Baby Bear's bed. When the bears return home, they are angry. In this softened version, Goldilocks helps clean up the house and makes the bears more food. They ask her to stay and eat with them. This story is a classic and has been translated into many languages. Its origin can be traced to England. Original versions of this story can be found in books listed in the Suggestions for Additional Reading (see page 171).

Unit Objectives

- to become familiar with the story

- to sequence events in a story

- to talk about one's feelings

- to make introductions and apologies

- to use regular verbs and the verb *to be* in the simple present tense

- to use predicate adjectives

- to answer questions with *who, what,* and *how* in the simple present tense

- to use singular and plural nouns

- to name the numerals 1–10 and to count to ten

- to count and label items with the correct numeral

Getting Ready to Read

Warm-Up

Show a picture of a real bear and ask students to identify the animal. Encourage children to tell what they know about bears. Then show them the illustration on page 26. Ask volunteers to tell what they see in the picture and what the bears are doing. Ask students if they know a story that goes with this picture. Allow any volunteers to share details about the story of Goldilocks and the three bears. If students are not familiar with the story, offer some details from the synopsis and encourage students to guess what happens when the bears come home. Students with limited conversation skills can draw pictures to show what they think will happen.

Vocabulary and Grammar Preview

Verbs	Nouns	Adjectives	Other
eat	*bears	angry	numerals 1–10
knock	bed	happy	
sit	chair	hot	
sleep	door	hungry	
tap	*feet (foot)	tired	
	food		

Grammatical Structures: simple present tense, singular and plural nouns, predicate adjectives

Decide which words and structures are new and which are review for your students. Follow the suggestions in Presenting the Story Units, Lesson One (pages 8–11) for appropriate vocabulary and grammar activities. Note that flashcards for the starred words are available on pages 156–164.

When practicing singular and plural noun forms, point out that *foot* has an irregular plural: *feet.*

Model the following conversation. Have pairs of students practice it. After they are familiar with saying the conversation, have them switch parts. Let volunteers act out the conversation for the class. As a follow-up activity, encourage children to talk about how they feel using the predicate adjectives *angry, happy, hot, hungry,* and *tired.*

Ten Tales for Teaching English © Good Year Books.

Child 1: *How do you feel?*

Child 2: *I feel (happy).*

Child 1: *(She) feels (happy).*

Monitor students' pronunciation of the final *s* on *feels,* checking for the /z/ sound.

Using the Student Pages

Presenting the Story

Follow the suggestions in Presenting the Story Units, Lessons Two and Three (pages 11–14) for reading and discussing parts 1 and 2 of "The Three Bears."

Presenting the Practice Page

As a warm-up, draw faces that illustrate *angry, hungry, happy,* and *tired* on the chalkboard. Talk about the faces and what they mean. Ask children, "How do you feel?" Encourage them to answer with, "I feel (tired)." Elicit additional adjectives that describe feelings, if appropriate. Draw a face for each one.

Focus children's attention on the practice page illustrations. Encourage them to talk about what is happening and about how each character feels. Give each child a copy of the practice page. Help students read the words in the word box and decide which word goes with each picture. Children who are already reading and writing in English can write the words under the pictures. Less advanced students may enjoy coloring the pictures.

As a closing activity, have pairs of children tell each other what is happening in the pictures.

Presenting the Application Page

The application page focuses on counting and naming the numerals 1–10. As a warm-up, write the numerals on the board and have students practice saying them in order and out of order. Ask them how many people are in their families and have them show the class the correct numeral.

Focus students' attention on the numerals at the top of the page and have them count from one to ten. Model the finger play and have students repeat it after you and act it out. When they are familiar with it, encourage them to come up and say it for the rest of the class. Children who are already reading in English can read the finger play as they act it out.

Next, focus students' attention on the illustrations at the bottom of the page. Have them tell you what is in each picture and count the objects. Show them how to write the correct numeral on the line. Have students complete the page with a friend or in groups.

As a closing activity, have them talk about the pictures and how they relate to the story. Ask questions such as "Whose (bowls) are these?" "What happens to the (bowls)?"

Presenting the Evaluation Page

As a warm-up for the evaluation page, show students the illustrations, flashcards, and any other visual aids from the story. Encourage them to tell what happened in the correct order. For children who are already reading and writing in English, write key sentences on the chalkboard for them. Next, show them the illustrations on this page. Have them tell what is happening in each picture and help them realize that the pictures are out of order. Model how the page should be completed, and then have students complete it independently.

As a closing activity, have children retell the story for a friend or the class using the illustrations on this page. Have students who are already writing in English write one or two sentences about each picture on a separate piece of paper.

Ten Tales for Teaching English © Good Year Books.

As part of your unit evaluation, ask students to complete the Now I Know page following the guidelines in Presenting the Story Units, Lesson Six (pages 15–16).

Additional Activities

Practice Introductions

Have children practice greeting each other by repeating the following conversation.

Child 1:   *Hello. My name is _____. Who are you?*
Child 2:   *Hello. I am _____.*

Practice Apologies

Have the children practice apologies using the following conversation.

Child 1:   *(Greg), you broke my (chair).*
Child 2:   *Oh, pardon me. I'm sorry.*

Draw and Tell

Give each child a piece of drawing paper. Have children draw pictures to show how they feel. Have them work with a partner and practice the following conversation.

Child 1:   *How do you feel?*
Child 2:   *I feel (happy).*

As a variation, have children draw four faces to depict the feelings *angry, hungry, happy,* and *tired.* Then let children take turns practicing the conversation, filling in the adjectives by holding up different pictures.

Write About It

Write the following word list and sentences on the chalkboard. Help children read and complete the sentences with the correct rhyming words. As a closing activity, ask volunteers to take turns reading the completed sentences.

four	feet	bear	dark	one

1. A family of bears sits down to eat.
   The bears are happy. They tap their _____.

2. Goldilocks sleeps. At a quarter to _____,
   The bears come back. They open the door.

3. She sees three beds and tries out each _____.
   She likes Baby's bed and says she is done.

4. Goldilocks sits and breaks Baby's chair.
   This chair is broken. Oh, poor Baby _____!

5. They go for a walk. They go to the park.

   They plan to come back when it is _____.

Ten Tales for Teaching English © Good Year Books.

The Three Bears, Part 1

A family of bears sits down to eat.
The bears are happy. They tap their feet.

"We're happy. We're hungry. Our food is here."
The three happy bears give a cheer!

"The food is so hot. We cannot eat."
The bears are not happy. They do not tap their feet.

"Let's go for a walk. Let's go to the park.
We can come back when it is dark."

So they all go out. Father shuts the door.
They plan to come back at a quarter to four.

A little girl goes to the door and she knocks.
"May I come in? I am Goldilocks."

No one is home. Goldilocks opens the door.
She eats Father's food. She says, "I want more."

She eats Mother's food. She eats Baby Bear's, too.
"I'm tired," she says, "but I know what to do."

Goldilocks sits in Father's big chair.
She says, "This chair's hard. It is for Father Bear."

Goldilocks sits in Mother's soft chair.
She says, "This chair's soft. It is for Mother Bear."

Tell what you know.

1. What do the bears do?
2. Who knocks at the door?
3. What does Goldilocks do?

The Three Bears, Part 2

Goldilocks sits and breaks Baby's chair.
This chair is broken. Oh, poor Baby Bear!

"I'm tired," she says. She walks up the stairs.
"Where are the beds for this family of bears?"

She sees three beds and she tries out each one.
"I like Baby's bed. Now I am done."

Goldilocks sleeps. At a quarter to four,
The bears come back. They open the door.

Father is angry. He asks, "Who is here?"
Goldilocks gets up and says, "Oh, dear!"

Father Bear goes to the bedroom to see.
Goldilocks says, "Oh, please, pardon me!"

She helps them clean up. She makes food to eat.
The bears are now happy. The bears tap their feet.

The three bears say, "Goldilocks, please stay to eat."
Goldilocks is happy. She taps her feet.

Tell what you know.

1. How does Goldilocks feel? What does she do?
2. How does Father Bear feel? What does he do?

Practice Page

How do they feel?

WORD BOX

angry   hungry   happy   tired

Talk to a partner. Tell what happens in each picture.

Ten Tales for Teaching English © Good Year Books.

Application Page

Say and count.

1   2   3   4   5   6   7   8   9   10

Say the finger play. Act it out.

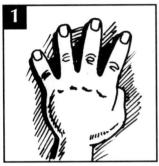 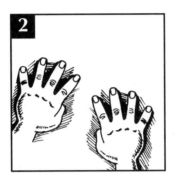 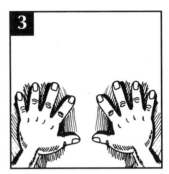

One, two, three, four. My family knocks at the door.

Five, six, seven, eight. I don't make them wait.

Open the door, nine, ten. Do it again!

Count. Write how many.

_____   _____   _____

Evaluation Page

Cut. Paste. Tell the story to a friend.

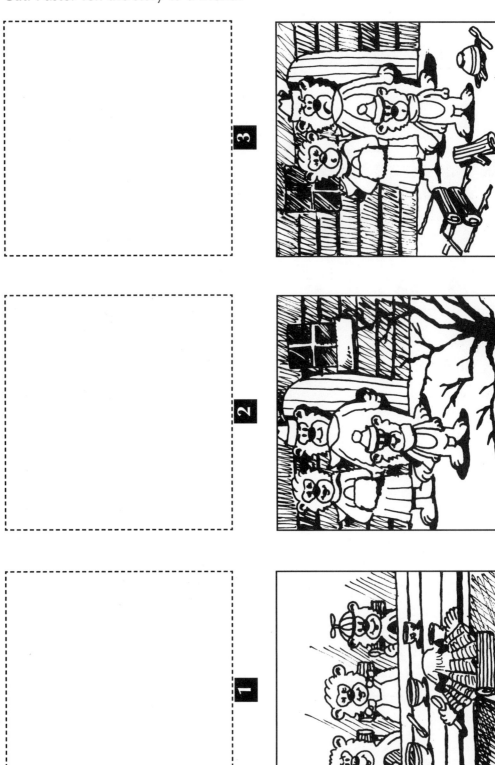

Overview

Story Synopsis

Cinderella lives with her stepmother and stepsisters. Cinderella cleans and cooks all day while they play. When the king invites everyone to a party, the stepmother and stepsisters go, leaving Cinderella at home to do more cleaning. A fairy visits Cinderella and gives her a new dress, shoes, and a carriage to go to the ball. She tells her to be home at midnight. Cinderella goes to the party, where she meets the prince and dances with him. As she is leaving at midnight, she loses her shoe. The prince returns with her shoe, and they get married. The stepmother and stepsisters are now left to cook and clean for themselves. This story is a classic and has been translated into many languages. Its origin can be traced to Europe. Original versions of this story can be found in books listed in the Suggestions for Additional Reading (see page 171).

Unit Objectives

- to become familiar with the story
- to sequence events in a story
- to talk about time
- to ask and answer questions about time
- to use regular verbs and the verb *to be* in the simple present tense
- to use predicate adjectives
- to use the preposition *at* when telling time
- to answer questions with *who, what,* and *how* in the simple present tense
- to name the numerals 1–12 and count to 12
- to tell time to the hour

Getting Ready to Read

Warm-Up

Show pictures or realia of a broom, bucket, soap, and sponge. Help students identify each item and tell how it is used. Then show students the illustration on page 39. Ask volunteers to tell what they see in the picture and what Cinderella is doing. Ask students to identify the other people in the illustration and talk about what those people are doing. Write the new vocabulary on the chalkboard. Invite volunteers to share what they know about the story of Cinderella. If students are not familiar with the story, offer some details from the synopsis and encourage students to guess what happens to Cinderella after the fairy helps her. Students with limited conversation skills can draw pictures to show what they think will happen.

Vocabulary and Grammar Preview

Verbs	Nouns	Adjectives	Other
bring	clock	mean	at
clean	dress		
cry	*fairy		
dance	floor		
invite	home		
marry	*king		
play	party		
ride	prince		
sit	shoe		
stay home	time		
wash			
work			

Grammatical Structures: simple present tense, predicate adjectives, preposition *at* used with time

Ten Tales for Teaching English © Good Year Books.

Decide which words and structures are new and which are review for your students. Follow the suggestions in Presenting the Story Units, Lesson One (pages 8–11) for appropriate vocabulary and grammar activities. Note that flashcards for the starred words are available on pages 156–164.

The application page (see page 42) presents telling time activities both for students who have not acquired much English and for students with more English ability. Use activities that best suit your students' needs.

Model the following conversation for children. Have students practice using the preposition *at* in sentences that tell time.

Child 1:   *What time do you (eat lunch)?*
Child 2:   *I (eat) at (12:00).*

As a follow-up activity, have students use the following substitutions in the modeled conversation: *go to school, eat dinner, eat breakfast, do my/your homework, go to bed, take a bath, get up.*

Using the Student Pages

Presenting the Story

Follow the suggestions in Presenting the Story Units, Lessons Two and Three (pages 11–14) for reading and discussing parts 1 and 2 of "Cinderella."

Presenting the Practice Page

For a warm-up, show students the flashcards for the characters in the story. Have students identify the characters and tell what each is doing. Have students retell the story using the flashcards. Then, give each student a copy of the practice page. Help them read the directions at the top and model cutting out the illustrations to make game cards. Have students work in pairs or groups to cut out the pictures on their practice pages. When they are finished, instruct them how to play one of the card games described on the next page. (Children in kindergarten might have trouble cutting out the pictures by themselves. If necessary, prepare the cards for them.) If there is time, have students color each game card.

Card Games

Matching Students can play this in pairs, groups, or as a class. Take two decks of cards, mix them up, and lay them face down on the table. Have children take turns choosing two cards. If the cards match, they keep them. If they don't, play goes to the next child. Encourage children to name the characters and what each does as they turn over the cards. The game is over when all the "matches" are found. The player with the most matches at the end of the game wins. As a closing activity, have each child talk about their cards.

Go Around Students can play this in groups of three or more. Use two decks of cards. Mix up the cards and deal them to students. Choose a player to start. Each child takes a turn choosing a card from the player on their right and tries to match a card that they are holding. If they match, they place the two cards face up on the table. When a player runs out of cards, the game ends. The player with the most matches at the end of the game wins. As a closing activity, have children talk about their cards, using the simple present tense.

Child: *Cinderella cooks.*
              Cinderella cleans. Cinderella loses her shoe.
              The prince gives Cinderella her shoe. Cinderella and the
              prince are happy.
              The stepmother and stepsisters clean.

Guess Who Choose a card and put it behind your back. Ask children, "Guess who?" Encourage them to use as much new vocabulary as possible and to answer in complete sentences. Continue by saying, "What does he/she do?" The player who guesses correctly then chooses the next card and asks, "Guess who?" As a closing activity, have each child talk about their favorite cards.

Act It Out Have students act out the story with puppets made from the flashcards. Paste the pictures of the characters on paper bags or glue craft sticks to the backs of the flashcards to create the puppets. Read the story using the puppets. Then ask volunteers to act out the story as you read it again. Have students practice the dialogues from the story as you narrate.

Ten Tales for Teaching English © Good Year Books.

Teacher: *Cinderella cleans. She washes the floor. When she brings them some food, they say,*

Children: *We want more.*

Presenting the Application Page

The application page focuses on telling time and naming the numerals 1–12. As a warm up, write the numerals 1–12 on the chalkboard and have students practice saying the numerals in order and out of order. Show them a copy of the completed clock and have them identify the numerals and the clock. Have them practice the following conversation.

Child 1:   *What time is it?*

Child 2:   *It's 12:00.*

Model when necessary.

Show students 12:00 on the clock and ask them what happened at 12:00 in the story. Help them understand that Cinderella had to be home from the party at this time.

Give each student a copy of the application page. Help them read the directions at the top, and model how to assemble the clock. Have students work in pairs or groups to assemble their clocks. After each clock is completed, have students set them to 12:00 and take turns telling what happened in the story at this time. As a closing activity, have students ask and tell what time it is using their clocks.

If children are familiar with numerals and ready to tell time, introduce this topic by having them point to each numeral on the clock as they name it. Model when necessary. Have them tell time to the hour, beginning with 12. Help them understand that twelve o'clock is the time Cinderella had to be home from the party. Continue with the rest of the hours by modeling each one first and have students repeat after you. Play a "show me" game by saying different times and having students set their clocks to match.

Presenting the Evaluation Page

As a warm-up for the evaluation page, show students the illustrations, flashcards, and any other visual aids from the story. Encourage them to tell what happened in the correct order. For children who are already reading and writing in English, write key sentences on the chalkboard for them.

Next, show students the illustrations on this page. Have them tell what happens in each picture. Help students read the directions at the top of the page. Model cutting out the illustrations, and show students how to put the pictures in the correct order to make a book. Give each child a copy of this page and some scissors. Have them put the illustrations in the correct order and staple them to create a book.

Do a "show me" activity. Repeat one of the dialogue lines from the story and have students hold up the page in their books that goes with the dialogue. Have children take turns describing what happens on each of the pages in their books. If there is time, have them color the pictures.

As a closing activity, have children retell the story for a friend or the class using the illustrations on this page. Have students who are already writing in English write one or two sentences about each picture on a separate piece of paper. If there is time, have students talk about their favorite and least favorite character/characters in the story.

As part of your unit evaluation, ask the students to complete the Now I Know page following the guidelines in Presenting the Story Units, Lesson Six (pages 15–16).

Additional Activities

Look!

You will need the cards found on the practice page for this unit. Place a number of playing cards on a table or the ledge of the chalkboard. Instruct children to close their eyes. Remove one card, and have students open their eyes. Say, "Look! What's missing?" "Who's missing?" Encourage students to say as much as they can about the missing picture. As a closing activity, have students put the pictures in the correct order to retell the story. As they are doing this, have them tell what is happening in each picture.

Write About It

For this activity, you will need the flashcards from the practice page. Have children choose three flashcards and sequence them in the order in which they happened in the story. Have children write a sentence for each illustration. For students who have not acquired much English, have them use a copy of the story to find sentences that correspond with the pictures. If possible, have students paste the pictures on a piece of paper and write the sentences under them. As a closing activity, ask volunteers to share their work with the rest of the class.

Cinderella, Part 1

Cinderella is a girl. She's pretty and sweet.
She lives in a house on Second Street.

She lives with her stepsisters and stepmother, too.
They all live together. Do you know what they do?

Cinderella works at home all day.
Her stepsisters and stepmother stay home. They play.

Cinderella cleans. She washes the floor.
When she brings them some food, they say, "We want more!"

The King in the palace says, "Parties are fun.
Let's have a party. Invite everyone."

The stepmother and stepsisters say, "We can go."
Cinderella asks, "Can I?" They say, "No!"

"You have to stay home. You have to clean."
Cinderella thinks they are very mean.

Cinderella stays home. She sits and she cries.
The stepmother and stepsisters just say, "Good-by."

Tell what you know.

1. What does Cinderella do?
2. What does the stepmother do?
3. What do the stepsisters do?

Ten Tales for Teaching English © Good Year Books.

Cinderella, Part 2

A fairy comes in. "Cinderella, my dear,
Sit down beside me. Please, sit right here.

"I can help you. I know that you want to go, too.
I'll give you a new dress and two pretty shoes.

"Here is a carriage to ride in, my dear.
At 12:00 midnight, come right back here."

Cinderella dances. She meets the Prince, too.
When she leaves at 12:00, she loses her shoe!

The Prince comes to see her. He brings her lost shoe.
He asks Cinderella to marry him, too!

Cinderella and the Prince go to the palace that day.
"We are so happy," the Prince and Cinderella say.

The stepmother and stepsisters stay home. They can't play.
Cinderella is gone. Now they work every day.

Tell what you know.

1. When does Cinderella go home?
2. What does the Prince do?
3. What do the stepmother and stepsisters do now?

Ten Tales for Teaching English © Good Year Books.

Practice Page

Cut. Let's play cards!

Application Page

Let's tell time.

Cut. Make a clock.

You will need one of these.

Ten Tales for Teaching English © Good Year Books.

Evaluation Page

Cut. Make a book. Tell the story.

The Little Red Hen

Story Synopsis

The Little Red Hen is a very hard worker. She has three friends: a duck, a cat, and a dog. They all like to play instead of work. One day, the Little Red Hen finds some wheat and asks her friends to help plant it. They refuse, so she plants it by herself. When it is time to cut the wheat, take it to the miller, and bake the bread, she asks her friends to help her. Each time they refuse to help, so the hen does all of these things herself. When the bread is baked, her friends want to help the Little Red Hen eat it. She tells them that they have to work if they are going to eat. She tells them to plant some wheat, grow it, cut it, and then make their own bread. This story is a classic and has been translated into many languages. Its origin can be traced to England. Original versions of this story can be found in books listed in the Suggestions for Additional Reading (see page 171).

Unit Objectives

- to become familiar with the story

- to sequence events in a story

- to talk about plants and how they grow

- to talk about animals and identify them

- to use regular verbs and the verb *to be* in the simple present tense

- to answer questions with *who, what,* and *how* in the simple present tense

- to use *will* to make requests or promises

- to use *won't* to show refusal

Getting Ready to Read

Warm-Up

Show children pictures or realia of flour, bread, and butter. Help them identify and talk about the items. Invite volunteers to tell what you do with each one. Help students talk about the process of making bread and what they like to eat with it. Show them the illustration on page 52, and help them identify the wheat, flour, and bread in the picture. Help them understand how wheat gets made into bread. Help students find and identify all of the animals on the page. Elicit what students know about the animals. Encourage them to tell what each animal does and is doing. Write key vocabulary on the chalkboard. Ask volunteers to share what they know about the story of the Little Red Hen. If students are not familiar with the story, offer some details from the synopsis and encourage students to guess who makes the bread and who eats it. Students with limited conversation skills can draw pictures to show what they think will happen.

Vocabulary and Grammar Preview

Verbs	Nouns	Adjectives	Other
bake	*bread	done	will
cut	*cat	little	won't
eat	*dog		
go	*duck		
pick	*flour		
plant	friend		
play	*hen		
run	miller		
water	plant		
work	*sun		
	water		
	*wheat		

Grammatical Structures: simple present tense, *will* for requests and promises, *won't* for refusals

Decide which words and structures are new and which are review for your students. Follow the suggestions in Presenting the Story Units, Lesson One (pages 8–11) for appropriate vocabulary and grammar activities. Note that flashcards for the starred words are available on pages 156–164.

This unit presents *will* in a very simple form. It is important for children to understand the function of this lexical frame, but they do not need to understand the function of *will* when it is used for the future tense.

Model the following conversation. Have pairs of students practice it. After they are familiar with saying the conversation, have them switch parts. Let volunteers act out the conversation for the class.

Child 1: *Will you help me (plant the wheat)?*
Child 2: *No, I won't./Yes, I will.*

As a follow-up activity, encourage children to use the following substitutions in the conversation: *work, cut the wheat, make the bread, eat the bread.*

Practice requests, promises, and refusals.

Using the Student Pages

Presenting the Story

Follow the suggestions in Presenting the Story Units, Lessons Two and Three (pages 11–14) for reading and discussing parts 1 and 2 of "The Little Red Hen."

Presenting the Practice Page

As a warm-up, show students pictures of a duck, hen, cat, and dog. Have children identify each one and tell what each does in "The Little Red Hen." Write each animal word on the chalkboard and help students read them. Then, show the illustration on page 52. Have students find the animals and read the corresponding word for each. Have them retell the story, using the illustration as a guide.

Ten Tales for Teaching English © Good Year Books.

Show students a copy of the practice page, and have them take turns pointing to the animal as you say its name. Tell them that they are going to listen, then circle the animal that you name. Help students read the directions at the top of the practice page. Model how the page is to be completed.

1. Circle the duck.

2. Circle the hen.

3. Circle the cat.

4. Circle the dog.

Focus the children's attention on the questions below the pictures. Ask the questions, and have students point to the correct pictures as they answer. Ask volunteers to identify the animals.

As a closing activity, encourage children to talk about their favorite animals from the story.

Presenting the Application Page

The application page focuses on the process of growing a plant. As a warm-up, show visual aids or realia for seeds, a watering can, and a plant. Help students identify each and talk about planting a seed and helping it grow. Write key vocabulary on the chalkboard. Help children sequence the vocabulary to show the process of planting.

Show students a copy of the application page. Have them talk about what is happening in the pictures on each leaf. Help them see and understand that the pictures are out of order. Show students how to cut out and paste the leaves on the plant to show the correct sequence of events. Give each student a copy of this page. Help them read the directions at the top. Then, have children work in pairs or groups to complete the page. When they are finished, ask volunteers to tell what is happening in each picture and talk about the process of planting. As a closing activity, have students talk about how the pictures relate to the story: "The Little Red Hen plants the seeds/wheat," and so on.

Presenting the Evaluation Page

As a warm-up for the evaluation page, show students the illustrations, flashcards, and any other visual aids from the story. Encourage them to tell what happened in the story. For children who are already reading and writing in English, write key sentences on the chalkboard for them. Then, give each student a copy of the evaluation page. Have them tell what is happening in each picture, and help them realize that the pictures are out of order. Read the directions aloud, and model how the page should be completed. Then, have students complete the page independently.

As a closing activity, have children retell the story for a friend or the class using the illustrations on this page. Have students who are already writing in English write one or two sentences about each picture on a separate piece of paper.

As part of your unit evaluation, ask students to complete the Now I Know page following the guidelines in Presenting the Story Units, Lesson Six (pages 15–16).

Additional Activities

Farm Animals

Teach children the sounds that these animals make: duck/quack, cat/meow, hen/cheep, dog/bow-wow. Teach children the song, "Old MacDonald Had a Farm" using the animals from the story. This song is presented in Unit 5, "The Hungry Goat." Check the section, Presenting the Application Page, in that unit for suggestions on teaching and presenting this song.

Planting

Plant seeds (lima bean seeds work well) with children. Review the application page as a warm-up. You will need paper cups, potting soil, water, and some bean seeds for this activity. Model how to fill the cups, plant the seeds, and water them. Have students work in groups to complete the activity. Encourage them to tell how this activity relates to the story. Place the seed cups on a windowsill and watch/monitor their growth. Have students measure and record the height of their plants. When the plants are big enough, children can take them home and share their work with their families.

The Moral

As a warm-up, review the story with students using the illustrations from the story and any additional visual aids or realia. Ask children who their favorite character is and help them tell you why. Accept all reasonable answers as students' opinions will vary. Write key words on the chalkboard for them. Next, ask them what they learned from the story. Help them talk about the moral and understand what the Little Red Hen meant when she said, "You have to work, too. You have to help work." As a closing activity, ask volunteers to share what they have learned from the story.

Put on a Play

Teach students the dialogue by holding up the appropriate visual aid for each question and modeling the answer. Have them provide the answer as you ask the question. Next, show them the appropriate visual aid and have them provide the question as you say the answers. When they are familiar with the dialogue, divide the class into groups and assign them parts from the story. Have them practice, and then have each group put on a play for the rest of the class.

Hen:	*Will you help me plant the wheat?*
Dog, Cat, Duck:	*We won't. (I won't.)*
Hen:	*Will you help me cut the wheat?*
Dog, Cat, Duck:	*We won't. (I won't.)*
Hen:	*Will you help me take the wheat to the miller?*
Dog, Cat, Duck:	*We won't. (I won't.)*
Hen:	*Will you help me bake the bread?*
Dog, Cat, Duck:	*We won't. (I won't.)*
Hen:	*Will you help me eat the bread?*
Dog, Cat, Duck:	*We will. (I will.)*
Hen:	*No, you won't. You didn't help!*

As a closing activity, ask volunteers to retell the story in their own words.

Writing Questions

As a warm-up, show students the illustrations/visual aids from the story and have them retell the story using their own words. Write the following questions on the chalkboard and help students read them. Show them a copy of the evaluation page, and help them decide which questions go with the pictures. Help children sequence the questions so they are in the correct order. As a closing activity, have students take turns asking and answering the questions.

1. Who will help me plant the wheat?

2. Who will help me work?

3. Who will help me cut the wheat?

4. Who will help me make the bread?

5. Who will help me eat the bread?

Ten Tales for Teaching English © Good Year Books.

The Little Red Hen, Part 1

The Little Red Hen works so hard every day.
There is so much to do. There is no time to play.

The hen has three friends. The friends like to play.
The dog and the cat and the duck play all day.

One day, the Little Red Hen finds some wheat.
"Come, let's plant it. Let's make bread to eat."

The hen asks her friends, "Will you help me plant wheat?"
Her friends say, "We won't, but we will help you eat."

The Little Red Hen works all day in the sun.
She plants all the wheat and then she is done.

The hen works each day. The wheat grows so high.
The hen says, "Let's cut it." Her friends ask her, "Why?"

"The miller makes flour. Let's cut down the wheat.
We can make bread, then we can eat."

The hen asks her friends, "Will you help cut the wheat?"
Her friends say, "We won't, but we will help you eat."

Tell what you know.

1. What does the hen do?
2. What do the cat, dog, and duck do?

Ten Tales for Teaching English © Good Year Books.

Ten Tales for Teaching English © Good Year Books.

The Little Red Hen, Part 2

The Little Red Hen works all day in the sun.
She cuts down the wheat and then she is done.

"Will you go to the miller to make flour from the wheat?"
"We won't," say her friends, "but we will help you eat."

She takes all the wheat to the miller that day.
The miller makes flour. What does the hen say?

The Little Red Hen asks, "Will you help make the bread?"
Her friends say, "We won't." The friends shake their heads.

The Little Red Hen works all day. When she's done,
Her friends smell the bread. Her friends start to run.

The dog and the cat and the duck say, "Let's go!
It's time to eat bread." The hen says, "Oh, no!"

"You have to work, too. Go plant some wheat.
Grow it. Then cut it. Then make bread to eat."

"You have to help work." Then the hen says, "Now, go."
The dog and the cat and the duck say, "Oh, no!"

Tell what you know.

1. What does the Little Red Hen say?
2. What do the dog, the cat, and the duck say?
3. Who eats the bread?

Practice Page

Listen. Circle.

1.   hen   cat   dog   duck

2.   duck   hen   cat   dog

3.   cat   duck   hen   dog

4.   hen   duck   dog   cat

Who works?

Who plays?

Who eats?

Ten Tales for Teaching English © Good Year Books.

Application Page

Tell what happens. Cut and paste.

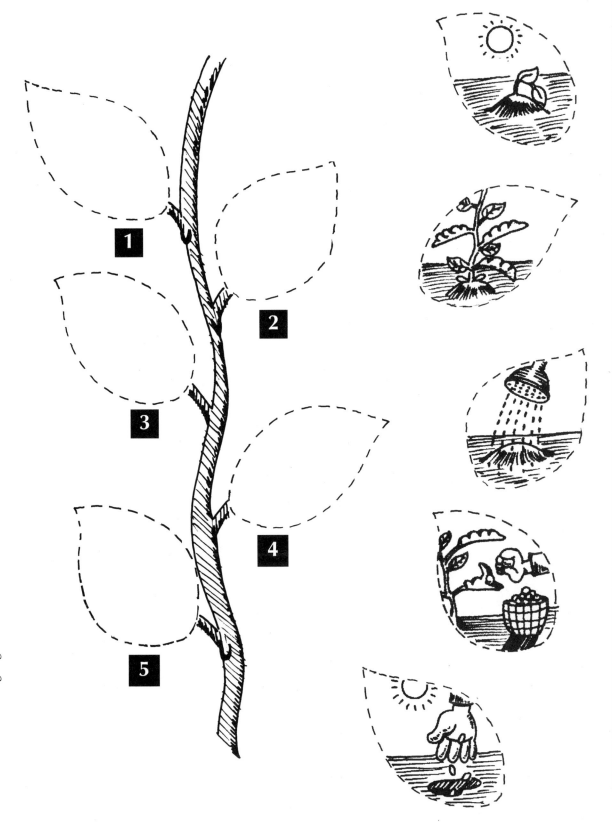

Evaluation Page

What does the Little Red Hen do?
What do the cat, dog, and duck do?

Cut. Paste the pictures to tell the story.

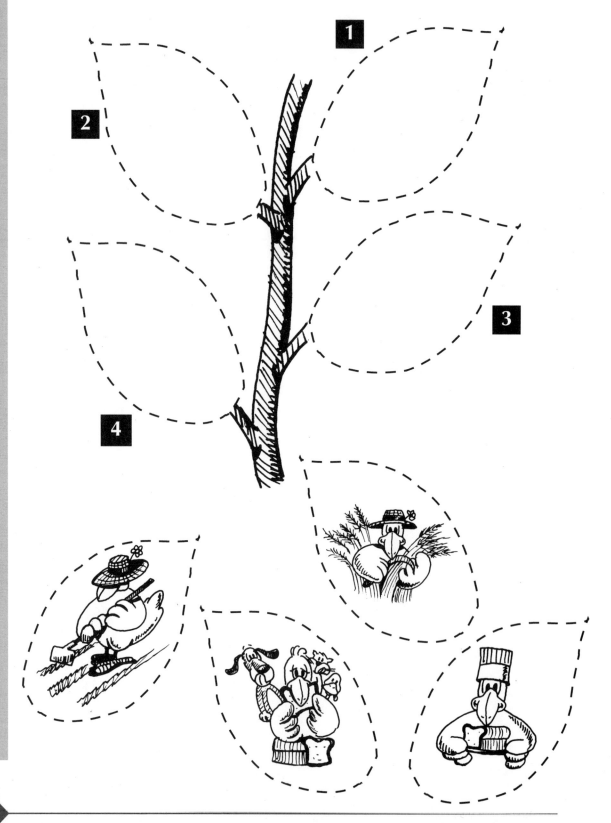

Ten Tales for Teaching English © Good Year Books.

OverView

Story Synopsis

A man asks his wife to make him a bun to eat. After the bun is baked, it comes to life and runs away. On the way, it meets a small rabbit, a fat wolf, a big bear, and a fast fox. As the bun runs along, it sings a song about how it cannot be caught. When the bun meets the quick fox, the fox asks the bun to come closer because he cannot hear the song. When the bun does, the fox eats it. In the end, the man is still hungry and asks his wife to make him something to eat and says that he would rather eat some meat, not a bun. This story comes from Russia, but variations can be found in many languages, including English ("The Gingerbread Boy") and Scandinavian ("The Pancake").

Unit Objectives

- to become familiar with the story

- to sequence events in a story

- to act out the story

- to talk about baby animals and their mothers

- to use regular verbs and the verb *to be* in the simple present tense

- to use predicate adjectives

- to answer questions with *who, what,* and *how* in the simple present tense

- to use the modal *can* in the affirmative and negative forms

Getting Ready to Read

Warm-Up

Show pictures of a rabbit, a bear, a wolf, and a fox. Encourage children to tell what they know about these animals. Then show them the illustrations on pages 64 and 65. Ask volunteers to tell what they see in the pictures and what the animals are doing. Help them find and identify the bun and talk about what it is and what it is doing. Ask students if they know a story that goes with these pictures. Allow volunteers to share details about the story, "Catch the Bun," or a similar story, such as "The Gingerbread Man" or "The Pancake." If students are not familiar with the story, offer some details from the synopsis and encourage students to guess what happens when the bun meets the fox. Students with limited conversation skills can draw pictures to show what they think will happen.

Vocabulary and Grammar Preview

Verbs	Nouns	Adjectives	Other
catch	*bear	big	cub
eat	*bun	fast	pup
make	butter	fat	bunny
meet	*feet	small	
run	*flour		
sing	*fox		
sit	man		
	*milk		
	*rabbit		
	wife		
	woman		
	*wolf		

Grammatical Structures: simple present tense, predicate adjectives, modal *can*

Decide which words and structures are new and which are review for your students. Follow the suggestions in Presenting the Story Units, Lesson One (pages 8–11) for appropriate vocabulary and grammar activities. Note that flashcards for the starred words are available on pages 156–164.

The predicate adjectives can be presented using visual aids. Draw pictures of the words and their opposites to show contrast (see next page for suggestions).

Ten Tales for Teaching English © Good Year Books.

| fat/skinny | big/small | fast/slow |

After children are familiar with the vocabulary, play a guessing game. Act out an adjective and have students guess the word. The student who guesses correctly gets to act out the next adjective.

Practice using the modal *can* and its negative form *cannot*. As a warm-up, say: "I can see you." Cover your eyes and say, "I cannot see you." Help students understand the meanings of these two sentences and continue with other examples. Model the following conversation and have children practice it with you.

Child 1:   *What can you do?*
Child 2:   *I can (run).*

Child 1:   *What can he/she do?*
Child 3:   *He/she can (run).*

As a follow up activity, encourage children to ask and answer questions that fit this pattern. Some possible substitutions are: *work, write, read, jump, hop,* and *climb.*

Help students understand that, in the third person singular form, there is no final *s* needed for the word *can.*

The application page has additional vocabulary with which students may not be familiar. Present the new words, *pup, cub,* and *bunny* with visual aids and have students practice saying and identifying the animals as a warm-up. Once they are familiar with the new vocabulary, have them complete the application page on page 67. Check the section, Presenting the Application Page, for specific directions.

Note that *who,* instead of *whom,* is used in the objective case in the story to allow a more natural flow of spoken language. *Whom* is most often used in the written form whereas *who* is most often used in conversation.

Using the Student Pages

Presenting the Story

Follow the suggestions in Presenting the Story Units, Lessons Two and Three (pages 11–14) for reading and discussing parts 1 and 2 of "Catch the Bun."

Presenting the Practice Page

As a warm-up, use the flashcards to review the animals on this page. Have children talk about what each animal does in the story. Help students review the sequence in which the animals appear in the story. Then, show students a copy of the practice page, and have them talk about the pictures and the story. Help students read the directions at the top of the page and model how to follow the maze. Have children work in pairs or groups to complete the page. After they are finished, invite volunteers to show how they went through the maze. Encourage students to name the animals as they pass them in the maze and tell what the animals do in the story. As a closing activity, ask children questions about the story characters using the modal *can*.

Teacher:	*Can the bun run?*
Child:	*Yes, it can.*
Teacher:	*Can the bun sing?*
Child:	*Yes, it can.*
Teacher:	*Can the wolf catch the bun?*
Child:	*No, it cannot.*
Teacher:	*Can the man catch the bun?*
Child:	*No, it cannot.*

Presenting the Application Page

The application page focuses on naming animals and their babies. As a warm-up, show students pictures of baby animals and their mothers, and help them name the animals and talk about them. Then, show children the application page, and have them identify the pictures. Help students read the directions at the top of the page. Model the activity, and have

Ten Tales for Teaching English © Good Year Books.

students work in groups or pairs to complete the page. As a closing activity, have children share their work with the rest of the class and talk about how the pictures relate to the story.

Presenting the Evaluation Page

As a warm-up for the evaluation page, show students the illustrations, flashcards, and any other visual aids from the story. Encourage them to identify the characters and to tell what happened in the story. For children who are already reading and writing in English, write key sentences on the chalkboard for them. Next, show them the illustrations on this page, and have them identify each picture. Help students read the directions at the top of the page. Then, use prepared puppets with the following dialogue to act out the story.

The man:	*I cannot catch the bun!*
The bun:	*You cannot catch me. I am a fast bun.*
	You cannot catch me. Just watch me run!
The rabbit:	*I cannot catch the bun!*
The bun:	*You cannot catch me. I am a fast bun.*
	You cannot catch me. Just watch me run!
The wolf:	*I cannot catch the bun!*
The bun:	*You cannot catch me. I am a fast bun.*
	You cannot catch me. Just watch me run!
The bear:	*I cannot catch the bun!*
The bun:	*You cannot catch me. I am a fast bun.*
	You cannot catch me. Just watch me run!
The fox:	*I can catch the bun! I can eat the bun!*

Show students how to cut out and prepare their puppets. Glue the pictures on paper bags or attach craft sticks to the backs.

Assign the parts of the bun and the animals, and have children practice the dialogue in groups. As a closing activity, have each group put on their puppet show for the class. Students who are in kindergarten might have trouble cutting out their puppets. Prepare the puppets for them before doing this activity. Students who are already reading and writing in English might enjoy writing their own puppet play.

As part of your unit evaluation, ask students to complete the Now I Know page following the guidelines in Presenting the Story Units, Lesson Six (pages 15–16).

Additional Activities

Favorite Pets and Animals

Have children talk about their favorite animals or pet. Encourage them to draw pictures and share them with the class. Students who are already writing in English can write one or two sentences about their pictures.

Make some Rabbit Food

Children will enjoy measuring, mixing, and serving this "rabbit food." Before serving, make sure no one is allergic to any of the ingredients.

½ cup of a favorite cereal
½ cup of a favorite seed or nut
½ cup of another favorite cereal
½ cup of raisins

Serve in paper cups.

Make Some Butter

Bring in some heavy cream and place it in a container with a secure lid. Have children take turns shaking the container until the cream becomes butter. Serve on "buns" such as crackers or bread.

Ten Tales for Teaching English © Good Year Books.

Write About It

Write the following word list and sentences on the chalkboard. Help children read and complete the sentences with the correct rhyming words. As a closing activity, ask volunteers to take turns reading the completed sentences.

hour	run	feet	meat

1. When the bun is all finished, when it is done,
   The bun starts to sing. The bun starts to ____.

2. The bun runs along. Who does he meet?
   He meets a small rabbit with very small _____.

3. The man tells his wife that he wants to eat.
   He doesn't want a bun, he wants _____.

4. His wife uses milk, some butter, and flour.
   She mixes, then bakes it, for only one _____.

Adjectives and Animals

As a warm-up, review the animals and the story with students. Help them describe how each animal looks.

the small rabbit with small feet

the fat wolf with fat feet

the big bear with big feet

Give each student a piece of drawing paper and have children draw their favorite animals from the story. Invite students to share their work with the class. Encourage them to use the adjectives before the nouns as indicated above.

Catch the Bun, Part 1

A man says to his wife, "I'm hungry, my sweet.
Can you make me a bun? I want to eat."

His wife uses milk, some butter, and flour.
She mixes, then bakes it, for only one hour.

When the bun is all finished, when it is done,
The bun starts to sing. The bun starts to run.

"You cannot catch me. I am a fast bun.
You cannot catch me. Just watch me run!"

"Catch it! Let's run! Run!" says the man.
The man and his wife run as fast as they can.

The bun runs along. Who does he meet?
He meets a small rabbit with very small feet.

The rabbit calls out, "Come here, Mr. Bun."
The bun starts to sing. The bun starts to run.

"You cannot catch me. I am a fast bun.
You cannot catch me. Just watch me run!"

The bun runs along. Who does he meet?
He meets a fat wolf with very fat feet.

The fat wolf calls out, "Come here, Mr. Bun."
The bun starts to sing. The bun starts to run.

"You cannot catch me. I am a fast bun.
You cannot catch me. Just watch me run!"

Ten Tales for Teaching English © Good Year Books.

Tell what you know.

1. What does the bun do?
2. What does the rabbit do?
3. What does the wolf do?

Catch the Bun, Part 2

The bun runs along. Who does he meet?
He meets a big bear with very big feet.

The big bear calls out, "Come here, Mr. Bun."
The bun starts to sing. The bun starts to run.

"You cannot catch me. I am a fast bun.
You cannot catch me. Just watch me run!"

The bun runs along. Who does he meet?
He meets a quick fox. The fox wants to eat.

The quick fox calls out, "Come here, Mr. Bun."
The bun starts to sing. The bun starts to run.

"You cannot catch me. I am a fast bun.
You cannot catch me. Just watch me run!"

The fox says, "Sit down. I will sit, too.
Then sing me your song. I cannot hear you."

The bun sits and sings. The bun doesn't run.
The fox is so quick. He eats up the bun!

The fox sits and sings, "I can catch you!
You silly bun, I am quick too!"

The man in his house asks his wife, "Can we eat?
But, please, not a bun! Can you make us some meat?"

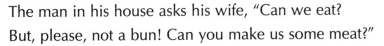

Tell what you know.
1. What does the bear do?
2. What does the fox do?
3. What does the man want to eat?

Practice Page

Follow the maze. Tell the story.

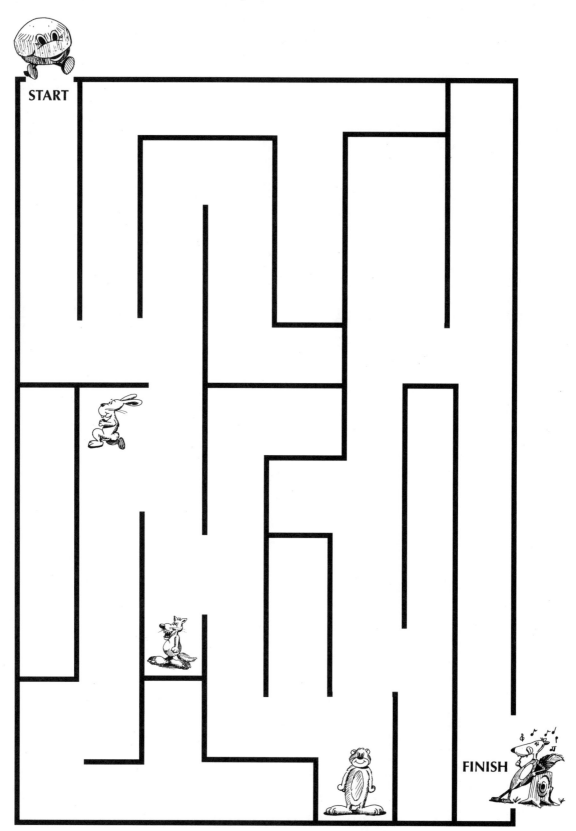

START

FINISH

Ten Tales for Teaching English © Good Year Books.

Application Page

Find the mother. Find the baby. Draw a line.

wolf

bunny

bear

wolf pup

rabbit

bear cub

What is your favorite animal? Tell a friend about it.

Evaluation Page

Make puppets. Act out the story.

OverView

Story Synopsis

A hungry goat happens upon a pepper garden. When he starts to eat, the farmer tells him to get out. The goat continues to eat and tells the farmer, "No!" The farmer enlists the help of some barnyard friends: a rooster, a dog, a cow, and an ant. Each animal asks the goat to leave, but the goat refuses and continues to eat the peppers. When the farmer finally asks the ant to help him, the ant climbs on the goat's back and bites him. The goat leaves the garden. The farmer thanks the ant for its help. This story comes from Mexico. Variations can be found in New Mexico and other Hispanic cultures.

Unit Objectives

- to become familiar with the story

- to sequence events in a story

- to act out the story

- to ask and answer questions about how one feels

- to use regular verbs and the verb *to be* in the simple present tense

- to use predicate adjectives

- to answer questions with *who, what,* and *how* in the simple present tense

- to give and act out commands

- to say animal sounds

- to sing a song

Getting Ready to Read

Warm-Up

Show pictures of a real goat, dog, cow, rooster, horse, and ant, and ask students to identify each animal. Encourage children to tell what they know about each. Then show them the illustration on page 78. Ask volunteers to tell what they see in the picture and what the animals are doing. Ask students if they know a story that goes with this picture. Allow volunteers to share details about the story of the Hungry Goat. If students are not familiar with the story, offer some details from the synopsis and encourage students to guess which animal helps the farmer. Students with limited conversation skills can draw pictures to show what they think will happen.

Vocabulary and Grammar Preview

Verbs	Nouns	Adjectives	Other
eat	*ant	great	slow
go	*cow	hungry	softly
	*dog	quiet	bah
	*farmer	sweet	bow-wow
	garden		cock-a-doodle-do
	*goat		moo
	*horse		neigh
	*peppers		Ouch!
	*rooster		No!
			Oh, no!

Grammatical Structures: simple present tense, commands, predicate adjectives

Decide which words and structures are new and which are review for your students. Follow the suggestions in Presenting the Story Units, Lesson One (pages 8–11) for appropriate vocabulary and grammar activities. Note that flashcards for the starred words are available on pages 156–164.

Slow and *slowly* are both correct forms for this adverb.

Use the playing cards on the practice page as visual aids to help children practice saying the names of the characters and the sounds that they make. After children are familiar with the characters, play charades. Have them take turns acting out how each animal looks, walks, and so on. The player who guesses first acts out the next animal.

Ten Tales for Teaching English © Good Year Books.

After children have learned the names of the animals, have them practice making the corresponding sounds. Each language depicts animal sounds differently. Encourage students to share with the class the sounds that the animals make in their native languages. After they are familiar with the animal names and sounds, play a game. Ask them to make the sounds of the animals you name. Then ask them to say the names of the animal sounds you make. As a closing activity, have students take turns naming and making the animal sounds.

Model the following conversation. Have pairs of students practice it. After they are familiar with saying the conversation, have them switch parts. Let volunteers act out the conversation for the class. As a follow-up activity, have students draw pictures of their favorite animals. Encourage them to make the sound for their favorite animal as they share their work with the rest of the class.

Child 1:   *What does a (cow) say?*
Child 2:   *A cow says (moo).*

Model the following conversation to help students practice using the simple present tense and predicate adjectives. Have students work in pairs. After they are familiar with saying the conversation, have them switch parts. Let volunteers act out the conversation for the class. As a follow-up activity, encourage children to talk about how they feel and what they do using the predicate adjectives and verb combinations: *happy/play, sad/cry, angry/yell, thirsty/drink,* and *hungry/eat.* Write these combinations on the chalkboard for students.

Child 1:   *How do you feel?*
Child 2:   *I feel (happy).*
Child 1:   *What do you do?*
Child 2:   *I (play).*

Teacher: *What does (he/she) do?*
Child 3:   *(He/She) (plays).*

Monitor students' pronunciation of the final *s* on *feels,* checking for the /z/ sound. Use the minimal pair activity on page 9 in the section, Presenting the Story Units.

To help students practice saying and responding to commands, model and act out the following conversation. Have pairs of students practice it. After they are familiar with saying the conversation, have them switch parts. As a closing activity, let volunteers act out the conversation for the class.

Child 1:   *Get out of my garden, please.*
Child 2:   *(acts out the command)*

Use the following substitutions: *eat the peppers, don't eat the peppers, walk to the door, sit down, jump, stand, hop, close your eyes, open your eyes, touch your nose,* and so on.

Using the Student Pages

Presenting the Story

Follow the suggestions in Presenting the Story Units, Lessons Two and Three (pages 11–14) for reading and discussing parts 1 and 2 of "The Hungry Goat."

Presenting the Practice Page

As a warm-up, show students the flashcards for the characters from this story. Encourage them to talk about what happened in the story and to tell what each character did. Write key vocabulary on the chalkboard for students. Help them retell the story in the correct sequence, using the flashcards and words on the chalkboard as a guide.

Ten Tales for Teaching English © Good Year Books.

Show students the practice page illustrations, and have them talk about the pictures and identify the characters and the sounds that they make. Read the directions aloud and model how to cut out the cards. Give each student a pair of scissors and a copy of this page and have them cut out the pictures in pairs or groups. Choose a game from the suggestions below. Students in kindergarten might have trouble cutting out the pictures. If necessary, prepare the cards for them.

Cut and Paste As a warm-up, have students talk about the pictures. Elicit as much new vocabulary as possible and help them draw on past experiences and knowledge. Show them how to paste the pictures of the characters in the order in which they appear in the story. Make a completed copy available for children to use as a model. As a closing activity, ask volunteers to retell the story, using the pictures as a guide.

Mix Up As a warm-up, have children talk about the pictures. Give them the opportunity to talk about the animals and help them relate their own experiences to what happened in the story. Place the cards on a table or ledge of the chalkboard in the order in which they appeared in the story. Model how to retell the story using the cards as a guide. Have students close their eyes. Mix up the cards. Have children work as a group to sequence the cards. The game can also be played using two teams. The first team to correctly sequence the cards and retell the story wins. As a closing activity, have children choose their favorite character and tell what it did in the story.

Act It Out: Using Commands Have children make puppets from the flashcards by either gluing them on paper bags or attaching craft sticks to the backs of the illustrations. Read the dialogue and have students use the flashcards to act out what is happening. Model and practice the dialogue with students. When they are familiar with it, have them work in groups to practice their play. As a closing activity, have each group put on a puppet show for the class. Students who have acquired more English might enjoy writing their own dialogues and then acting them out for the rest of the class.

Farmer:	*Get out of my garden. Go, goat, go!*
Goat:	*Give me your peppers. Don't say, "No!"*
Rooster:	*Cock-a-doodle-do. Go, goat, go!*
Goat:	*Give me the peppers. Don't say, "No!"*
Dog:	*Bow-wow, bow-wow. Go, goat, go!*
Goat:	*Give me your peppers. Don't say, "No!"*
Cow:	*Moo, moo, moo. Go, goat, go!*
Goat:	*Give me your peppers. Don't say, "No!"*
Horse:	*Neigh, neigh, neigh. Go, goat, go!*
Goat:	*Give me your peppers. Don't say, "No!"*
Ant:	*Watch me now. I am quiet and slow.*
Goat:	*Ouch! Now I think it is time to go!*
Farmer:	*Little ant, please stay. I want to thank you.*
Ant:	*You're welcome. I'm small, but I know what to do.*

Charades Use the animal flashcards or the illustrations on the practice page. Place them in a pile, face down, on the table. Model how the game is played. Have a child pick a card and act out how the animal walks, moves, and sounds. The first child to guess the animal gets to choose the next card.

Presenting the Application Page

The application page focuses on the song "Old MacDonald's Farm." As a warm-up, show students visual aids for the dog, cow, rooster, and horse. Have them identify the animals and talk about the sounds they make. Encourage them to share the animal sounds from their native languages. Model the sounds that the animals make and have children practice them with you. When they are familiar with the sounds, model how the song "Old MacDonald's Farm" is sung. Say the first two lines and have children repeat them after you. Then have children sing the first part of the song. Present the rest of the song in the same way. When they are familiar with all the words for the song, have them sing it as a class. Children who are already reading in English can follow along and read the words to the song. Children who are not reading in English can use the illustrations as a guide. As a closing activity, ask students to think of other animals and substitute them in the song.

Ten Tales for Teaching English © Good Year Books.

Presenting the Evaluation Page

As a warm-up for the evaluation page, show students the illustrations, flashcards, and any other visual aids from the story. Encourage students to tell what happened in the correct order. For children who are already reading and writing in English, write key sentences on the chalkboard for them. Next, show them the illustrations on this page. Have students tell what is happening in each picture and help them realize that the pictures are out of order. Help children read the directions at the top of the page. Model how to complete the page, and then have students complete it independently.

As a closing activity, have children retell the story for a friend or the class using the illustrations on this page. Have students who are already writing in English write one or two sentences about each picture on a separate piece of paper.

As part of your unit evaluation, ask students to complete the Now I Know page following the guidelines in Presenting the Story Units, Lesson Six (pages 15–16).

Additional Activities

Farm Animals

Use visual aids to present other farm animals and the sounds they make. For example, cat/meow, duck/quack, pig/oink, chick/peep, sheep/bah, and so on. (Some of these animals are presented in "The Little Red Hen.") Have children take turns acting out the animal sounds and guessing what the animals are. This activity works well with the application page for this story.

Zoo Animals and Farm Animals

Use visual aids to present zoo animals. After children are familiar with this vocabulary, review the animals from this story. Set up and label two bags: Farm Animals and Zoo Animals. Have students take turns sorting the zoo and farm animal visual aids and putting them in the correct bags.

Reverse the procedure by calling out the names of the animals and having children find them in the bags.

Write About It

Write the following word list and poem on the chalkboard. Help children read and complete the sentences with the correct rhyming words. Have them copy and complete the poem on a separate piece of writing paper. As a closing activity, ask volunteers to take turns reading the completed sentences. As a follow up activity, have students illustrate the poem and tell what happened in their own words.

cow	dog	horse	farmer	rooster

Where are the animals?

"Bow-wow, bow-wow," says a ____ I know.
He runs away. Where does he go?

"Neigh, Neigh," says the ____. "Dog, where are you?"
Dog says, "In the garden. Please come in, too."

"Moo, moo, moo, moo," says a ____ I know.
She runs away. Where does she go?

"Cock-a-doodle-do," says the ____. "Cow where are you?"
Cow says, "I'm in the garden. Please come in, too."

"My animals are gone," says a ____ I know.
"Where are my animals? Where did they go?"

He looks in the garden and says, "Oh, no!"
Animals get out of my garden. Please go!"

The Hungry Goat, Part 1

A big billy goat walks. He's hungry, you know.
He says, "I want to eat. Where can I go?"

He walks and he says, "Look, what do I see?
I see peppers. Farmer, give them to me."

"These peppers are mine," says the farmer. "Now, go!"
The goat starts to eat and says, "No, no, no!"

The goat says, "I'm hungry. I want to eat.
These peppers are great. These peppers are sweet."

The farmer calls out to a rooster he sees,
"Get that goat out of my garden, please!"

"Cock-a-doodle-do," says the rooster. "Go, goat, go!"
The goat eats and eats. The goat just says, "No!"

The goat says, "I'm hungry. I want to eat.
These peppers are great. These peppers are sweet."

The farmer calls out to a dog that he sees,
"Get that goat out of my garden, please."

"Bow-wow," says the dog. "Go, goat, go."
The goat eats and eats. The goat just says, "No!"

The goat says, "I'm hungry. I want to eat.
These peppers are great. These peppers are sweet."

Tell what you know.

1. What does the farmer do?
2. What does the goat do?
3. What does the rooster say?
4. What does the dog say?

The Hungry Goat, Part 2

The farmer calls out to a cow that he sees,
"Get that goat out of my garden, please."

"Moo moo, moo, moo," says the cow. "Go, goat, go."
The goat eats and eats. The goat just says, "No!"

The goat says, "I'm hungry. I want to eat.
These peppers are great. These peppers are sweet."

The farmer calls out to a horse that he sees,
"Get that goat out of my garden, please."

"Neigh, neigh. Neigh, neigh," says the horse. "Go, goat, go!"
The goat eats and eats. The goat just says, "No!"

The goat says, "I'm hungry. I want to eat.
These peppers are great. These peppers are sweet."

The farmer calls out to an ant that he sees,
"Get that goat out of my garden, please."

The ant is so quiet. It doesn't say, "Go."
The ant walks up softly. The ant walks so slow.

The ant climbs up and, with all of his might,
The ant opens his mouth and takes a big bite.

"Bah. Ouch!" says the goat. "It's time to go!
I don't like this garden, oh no, oh no!"

"Ant," says the farmer, "I want to thank you.
I know you are small, but you know what to do!"

Tell what you know.

1. What does the cow say?
2. What does the horse say?
3. What does the ant do?
4. What does the goat do?

Practice Page

What do they do? What do they say?

Cut. Play cards.

Ten Tales for Teaching English © Good Year Books.

Application Page

Let's sing!

Old MacDonald's Farm

Old MacDonald had a farm,
e, i, e, i, o.
And on his farm he had a dog,
e, i, e, i, o.

With a bow-wow here,
and a bow-wow there.
Here a bow, there a bow,
everywhere a bow-wow.

Old MacDonald had a farm,
e, i, e, i, o.

Now sing the song for these animals too!

Evaluation Page
Tell the story. Cut and paste.

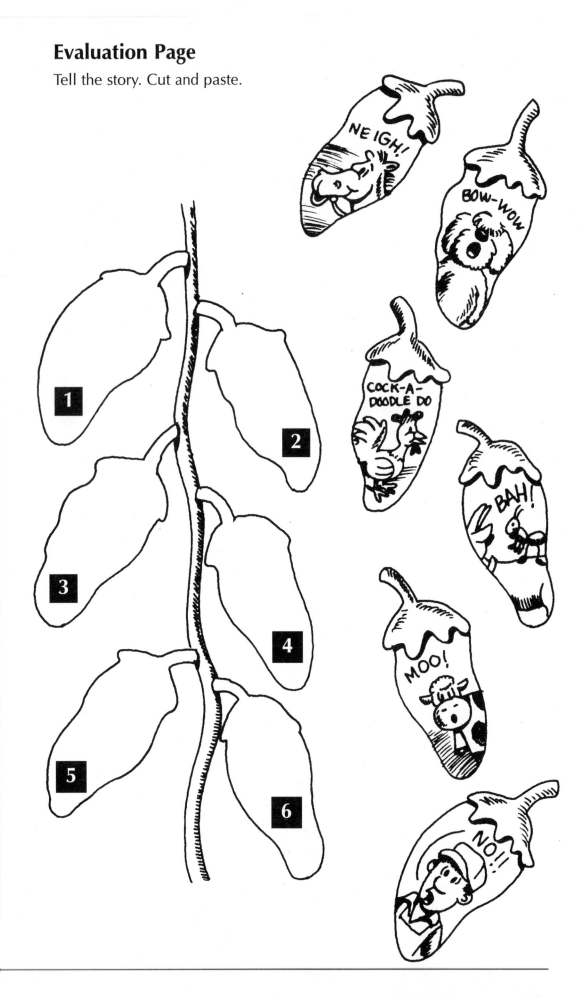

Ten Tales for Teaching English © Good Year Books.

OverVieW

Story Synopsis

Three billy goats, one small, one big, and one very big, see three fruit trees on the other side of the bridge. The goats think that the fruit looks delicious. The small billy goat wants to eat from the pear tree, the big billy goat wants to eat from the peach tree, and the very big billy goat wants to eat from the plum tree. A big ugly troll lives under the bridge and tries to keep them from crossing. The small and big billy goats talk the troll into letting them pass. They promise that the next goat will be bigger and, of course, make a better stew. When the very big billy goat crosses the bridge, he pushes the troll below the bridge. Now, the billy goats can cross the bridge whenever they want. The troll is now unhappy and leaves. This tale has its origin in Scandinavian literature. Original versions of this story can be found in books listed in the Suggestions for Additional Reading (see page 171).

Unit Objectives

- to become familiar with the story

- to sequence events in a story

- to talk about big and small things

- to ask and answer questions with *where* and use prepositions

- to answer questions with *who, what,* and *how* in the simple present tense

- to use regular verbs and the verb *to be* in the simple present tense

- to use the adjectives *big* and *small*

- to use the intensifier *very* to show more

- to give and execute commands

- to sequence by size

Getting Ready to Read

Warm-Up

Show a picture of a real goat and ask students to identify the animal. Encourage children to tell what they know about goats. Then show them the illustration on page 93. Ask volunteers how many goats they see in the picture. Ask them to tell what the goats are doing. Help them identify the troll, and ask them to describe the troll and to guess what he is doing. Help students identify the bridge, and ask them where the troll and goats are. Ask students if they know a story that goes with this picture. Allow volunteers to share details about the story of the three goats. If students are not familiar with the story, offer some details from the synopsis and encourage students to guess what happens when the goats try to cross the bridge. Students with limited conversation skills can draw pictures to show what they think will happen.

Vocabulary and Grammar Preview

Verbs	Nouns	Adjectives	Other
eat	billy *goat	big	slow
jump	bridge	gone	below
live	clip clop	quiet	in
stop	*peach	small	on
wait	*pear	ugly	over
	*plum	unhappy	very
	stew		3 (three)
	*tree		green
	*troll		orange
			purple
			red
			yellow

Grammatical Structures: simple present tense, adjectives *big* and *small*, intensifier *very*, commands, prepositions

Ten Tales for Teaching English © Good Year Books.

Decide which words and structures are new and which are review for your students. Follow the suggestions in Presenting the Story Units, Lesson One (pages 8–11) for appropriate vocabulary and grammar activities. Note that flashcards for the starred words are available on pages 156–164.

If children are unfamiliar with the verb *live*, show them a picture of a house or apartment building. Use familiar vocabulary and lexical frames such as, *I live in a house. I live in an apartment. I live here.* Encourage students to talk about where they live.

If students are unfamiliar with the verb *wait*, act it out by telling a volunteer to leave the room. Ask him/her to wait for you by the door. Show that it is necessary to stop and wait until you are ready.

Help children understand that a billy goat is a type of goat. Children who have acquired more English can be told that a billy goat is a male goat.

Model the prepositions by showing students items that they are familiar with in the classroom. Model *on* and *below* with a book, pencil, crayon, and so on. After students are familiar with these new words, have them take turns putting objects in the correct place as you say the preposition.

Teacher: *Put the pencil under the desk.*

Next, have children look again at the illustration on page 93. Have them talk about the bridge and act out walking over the bridge. Help students practice all of the prepositions by talking about the picture. Model the following sentences.

Teacher: *The goats walk over the bridge.*
           The troll is under the bridge.

Continue modeling the prepositions with the following conversation. Have students practice it in pairs. After they are familiar with the conversation, have them switch parts. Let volunteers act out the conversation for the class. As a follow-up activity, encourage children to talk about where different objects are in the classroom.

Child 1: *Where is the (book)?*
Child 2: *The (book) is (under) the (chair).*

Help children understand that the intensifier *very* helps an adjective mean "more." Model this lexical frame using visual aids and complete sentences such as, "It is a big pencil. It is a very big pencil." and so on. Show students a variety of big and very big objects and encourage them to talk about the objects using the adjective *big* and the intensifier *very*. As a closing activity, have children describe objects in the classroom that fit this pattern.

Have students practice giving and acting out commands with the following conversation. Have them practice it in pairs. After they are familiar with it, have them switch parts. Invite volunteers to give and act out the commands for the rest of the class.

Child 1: *Please (stand).*
Child 2: *(acts out the command)*

Additional verbs that fit this pattern are *stop, eat, jump, stop, wait, sit, walk, run, hop, look.*

Using the Student Pages

Presenting the Story
Follow the suggestions in Presenting the Story Units, Lessons Two and Three (pages 11–14) for reading and discussing parts 1 and 2 of "The Three Billy Goats."

Presenting the Practice Page
As a warm-up, draw pictures of known items that illustrate the adjectives *small, big,* and *very big.* Talk about the pictures. Ask children, "What is this?" Encourage them to answer with, "It's a (small) (pencil)." Elicit additional sentences with other known vocabulary that fit this model. Draw or write students' responses on the chalkboard for them to use as a reference.

Next, ask children to tell you about the story "The Three Billy Goats" and to talk about the characters. Help them describe the goats using the adjectives *small, big,* and *very big.* Focus children's attention on the practice page illustrations. Have them identify and describe the characters using the target vocabulary for this page. Model the conversation and have children practice it with you.

Child 1: *Who are you?*
Child 2: *I am the (small billy goat).*

Give each child a copy of the practice page on page 96. Help students read the directions and text in each picture. Have them cut out the pictures and practice the conversation with a partner using the illustrations. Less advanced students may enjoy coloring the pictures.

As a closing activity, help students read the directions for the bottom section of the practice page. Show students how to draw something small, big, and very big. Use a separate piece of paper. Have them share their work with the class using this conversation:

Child 1: *What is it?*
Child 2: *It's a (very big) (cat).*

Presenting the Application Page

The application page focuses on naming fruit and color words. As a warm-up, show students visual aids or realia for the words *peach, orange, plum, pear, banana,* and *apple.* Help children name each kind of fruit by modeling the following conversation for them. Have them practice it in pairs.

Teacher: *What is it?*
Child 1: *It is (a peach).*

If children are not familiar with color words, present them at this time. See Presenting the Story Units: Adjectives on page 11 for activities and suggestions.

Show students a copy of the practice page that is already colored and ask them, "What color is the peach?" Encourage them to respond using complete sentences, such as "The peach is orange."

Tell them that they are going to listen for directions, then color each piece of fruit as directed.

Teacher: *Color the peach orange.*
          Color the orange orange.
          Color the plum purple.
          Color the pear green.
          Color the banana yellow.
          Color the apple red.

Model the following conversation and have students practice it in pairs or groups.

Child 1:   *What color is the (apple)?*
Child 2:   *The (apple) is (red).*

Students who have acquired more English can write the sentences under the pictures. Write the sentences on the chalkboard, and help children read them. Then have students copy the sentences under the pictures.

As a closing activity, help students read the directions and conversation at the bottom of the page.
Ask and answer. "What is your favorite fruit?"
"I like (apples)."

Have students work in pairs to practice the conversation, using the plural forms of the nouns. Then, invite volunteers to act out the conversation for the rest of the class.

Presenting the Evaluation Page

As a warm-up for the evaluation page, show students the illustrations, flashcards, and any other visual aids from the story. Encourage them to tell what happened in the correct order. For children who are already reading and writing in English, write key sentences on the chalkboard for them. Next, show them the illustrations on the evaluation page. Have them tell what is happening in each picture. Show students how to cut out the pictures and make puppets by either pasting the pictures on paper bags or attaching the pictures to craft sticks. Model the following play for students using the puppets. Divide the class into groups and assign the parts of each character.

Small Billy Goat:	*I want to go over the bridge. I want to eat a pear. (acts out walking over the bridge)*
Troll:	*I am hungry. I want goat stew! (troll is hiding under the bridge)*
Small Billy Goat:	*Please let me go. Here comes my big brother.*
Troll:	*OK!*
Big Billy Goat:	*I want to go over the bridge. I want to eat a peach. (acts out walking over the bridge)*
Troll:	*I am hungry. I want goat stew! (troll is hiding under the bridge)*
Big Billy Goat:	*Please let me go. Here comes my very big brother.*
Very Big Billy Goat:	*I want to go over the bridge. I want to eat a plum. (acts out walking over the bridge)*
Troll:	*I am hungry. I want goat stew! (troll is hiding under the bridge)*
Very Big Billy Goat:	*Stop! (troll runs away)*
The Three Billy Goats:	*We go over the bridge every day!*

As part of your unit evaluation, ask the students to complete the Now I Know page following the guidelines in Presenting the Story Units, Lesson Six (pages 15–16).

Additional Activities

Where is it?

Use the illustrations from the evaluation page. Place them in obvious locations around the classroom using the propositions *on, below,* and *over.* Because the word *over* in the story is used in the context of "walking over the bridge," use it with similar meaning. Show children the illustration of the goat walking over the bridge and model the following conversation.

Teacher:	*Where does the goat go?*
Child:	*The goat goes over the bridge.*
Teacher:	*Where is the (troll)?*
Child:	*The troll is under the bridge.*

As a closing activity, have students generate similar conversations using the illustrations from the story.

Act It Out: Commands

As you say the following verbs, have children act them out. After they are familiar with the game, have them act out three verbs in succession. Verb suggestions: *jump, stop, eat, walk, wait, sit, stand.*

Play Stop!

Have students act out the following verbs until you say, "stop/don't stop." Students must listen carefully because if they make a mistake, they must sit down. The child who makes no mistakes is the winner. Verb suggestions: *jump, hop, walk, run, slow.*

Ten Tales for Teaching English © Good Year Books.

Rhyming Words Writing Activity

As a warm-up, review the story with children. Write the following sentences and word list on the chalkboard. Help students read the list and sentences and decide how to correctly fill in the answers. After children are familiar with the activity, give them a piece of writing paper. Erase the answers and have them complete the sentences with a partner. As a closing activity, ask volunteers to share their work with the class.

do	stop	day	slow

1. The big ugly troll hears a clip and a clop.
   He jumps on the bridge and wants the goat to _____.

2. The troll is unhappy. The troll goes away.
   The goats walk over the bridge every ____.

3. The very big billy goat wants to go,
   over the bridge. He doesn't go ____.

4. The big ugly troll wants some goat stew.
   The big ugly troll knows what to _____.

The Three Billy Goats

The Three Billy Goats, Part 1

Three billy goats live on a hill.
All of the billy goats are happy until…

They walk to a bridge. Do you know what they see?
They see lots of good things to eat on the trees.

The small billy goat says, "Look at that tree!
It has lots of pears. That one's for me!"

The big billy goat says, "Look at that tree!
It has lots of peaches. That one's for me."

The very big billy goat says, "Look at that tree!
It has lots of plums. That one's for me."

Below the bridge lives a big, ugly troll.
He's below the bridge in a very big hole.

The small billy goat says, "I want to go,
Over the bridge, quiet and slow."

The big ugly troll hears a clip and a clop.
He jumps on the bridge and yells, "Billy goat, stop!

"I am hungry," he says. "I want some goat stew."
The small billy goat says, "I know what to do."

He says to the troll, "Please let me go.
Wait for my brother. He's big, you know."

The troll says, "OK, I know what to do.
When the big goat comes, I can make lots of stew."

The small billy goat clips and he clops
Over the bridge and he doesn't stop.

He says, "I am hungry." He finds the pear tree.
He eats and he says, "This one's for me!"

Ten Tales for Teaching English © Good Year Books.

Tell what you know.

1. What do the billy goats want to eat?
2. What does the troll want to eat?

The Three Billy Goats, Part 2

The big billy goat says, "I want to go!
Over the bridge, quiet and slow."

The big ugly troll hears a clip and a clop.
He jumps on the bridge and yells, "Billy goat, stop!

"I'm hungry," he says. "I want some goat stew!"
The big billy goat says, "I know what to do."

He says to the troll, "Please let me go.
Wait for my brother. He's very big, you know."

The troll says, "OK, I know what to do.
When the very big goat comes, I can make lots of stew."

The big billy goat clips and he clops
Over the bridge and he doesn't stop.

He says, "I am hungry." He finds the peach tree.
He eats and he says, "This one's for me!"

The very big billy goat says, "I want to go.
Over the bridge. I don't walk slow."

The big ugly troll hears a clip and a clop.
He jumps on the bridge and yells, "Billy goat, stop!

"I am hungry," he says, "I want some goat stew!"
The very big billy goat knows what to do.

The very big billy goat pushes the troll
Below the bridge and into a hole!

The very big billy goat says, "Now *you* stop!"
The very big billy goat clips and he clops,

Over the bridge to the big plum tree.
He eats and he says, "This one's for me!"

The troll is unhappy. The troll goes away.
The goats walk over the bridge every day.

They walk with a clop and a clip and a clop.
The troll is gone and cannot say, "Stop!"

Tell what you know.

1. What does the very big billy goat do?
2. What does the troll do?

Practice Page

Ask and answer, "Who are you?"

Draw something small, something big, and something very big.
Use your own paper.

Application Page

Listen. Name each kind of fruit. Color.

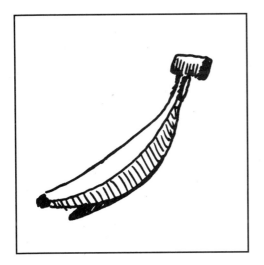 

Ask and answer. "What is your favorite kind of fruit?"

"I like _____s ."

Evaluation Page

Ten Tales for Teaching English © Good Year Books.

OverView

Story Synopsis

Anansi, the spider, is a trickster. One day he decides that he is hungry and wants to go hunting for eggs. He asks his friend, Firefly, to come along. They decide to go at night, and Firefly uses his light to help Anansi see in the dark. Anansi begins to take all of the eggs and leaves none for Firefly. Firefly becomes angry and goes home, leaving Anansi alone in the dark. Anansi finds Tiger, who offers to let him spend the night at his house. While they are at Tiger's house, Tiger makes Anansi cook all of the eggs, and then eats them. Anansi thinks there might be one more egg left. But, during the night, Tiger puts a lobster in the egg pot to trick Anansi. When Anansi puts his hand in the pot, the lobster bites him! On his way home, Anansi sees Firefly. Firefly doesn't want to talk or play with Anansi so Anansi is left alone with no friend and no eggs. This story's origin can be traced to Africa. It is part of the Ashanti Tribe literature as well as Jamaican literature.

Unit Objectives

- to become familiar with the story
- to sequence events in a story
- to use regular verbs and the verb *to be* in the simple present tense
- to act out the story
- to use predicate adjectives
- to use singular and plural nouns
- to answer questions with *who, what,* and *how* in the simple present tense
- to ask and answer questions with *how many* using count nouns
- to name the numerals 1–8
- to count and label items with the correct numeral/number word
- to use the possessive adjectives *mine* and *yours*
- to talk about possession
- to talk about and identify animals

Getting Ready to Read

Warm-Up

Show a picture of a real spider and ask students to identify the insect. Encourage children to tell what they know about spiders, what they look like, how many legs they have, where they live, and so on. Then show them the illustration on page 107. Ask volunteers to tell what they see in the picture and what the spider is doing. Help students find and identify the Firefly. Encourage children to tell what they know about fireflies and to talk about fireflies' "lights." Ask students if they know a story that goes with this picture. Allow volunteers to share details about the story of Anansi. If students are not familiar with the story, offer some details from the synopsis and encourage students to guess what happens to the eggs, Anansi, and the Firefly. Direct them to look at the Firefly's face to help them make their predictions. Students with limited conversation skills can draw pictures to show what they think will happen.

Vocabulary and Grammar Preview

Verbs	Nouns	Adjectives	Other
bite	*eggs	afraid	numerals/
eat	*firefly	dark	number words
fly	*hands	fun	1–8
play	home	hungry	mine
sing	light	none	yours
turn on	*lobster	scared	
wake up	night	shared	
walk	*tiger	tired	
	*toe		
	tonight		

Grammatical Structures: simple present tense, questions with *how many* and count nouns, singular and plural nouns, possessive adjectives *mine* and *yours*

Decide which words and structures are new and which are review for your students. Follow the suggestions in Presenting the Story Units, Lesson One (pages 8–11) for appropriate vocabulary and grammar activities. Note that flashcards for the starred words are available on pages 156–164.

Help students understand that fireflies come out at night and light up. Show them the illustration of the firefly on page 107. Say, "Firefly, turn on your light." Then, show them a copy of the same page with the firefly's tail colored yellow to show that the light "is on".

This unit includes adjectives that define emotions. If these words are new to your students, act them out and have children practice them with you. If they are familiar with the words, play a quick game of charades to review the words' meanings.

Next, model the following conversation. Have pairs of students practice lit. After they are familiar with saying the conversation, have children switch parts. Let volunteers act out the conversation for the class. As a follow-up activity, encourage children to talk about how they feel using the predicate adjectives *afraid/scared, tired, hungry.*

Child 1:   *How do you feel?*
Child 2:   *I feel (afraid).*
Child 1:   *(She) feels (afraid).*

Monitor students' pronunciation of the final *s* on *feels*, checking for the /z/ sound.

This unit also includes possessive adjectives. It is important for children to understand the meanings of these adjectives and to have opportunities to practice using these new words. Act out the words *mine* and *yours* so students understand their meanings in relation to themselves and the story.

Teacher: *Hold up your book and say: "This book is mine."*
Teacher: *Hold up a student's book and say: "This book is yours."*

Help students practice this pattern using objects in the classroom. Have them work in pairs, and then take turns saying this short conversation for the class.

Help students work with the singular and plural forms of the following nouns: *lobster(s)*, *firefly(ies)*, *tiger(s)*, *hand(s)*, *toe(s)*. See Presenting the Story Units: Nouns on pages 10–11, for suggestions on teaching and activities. Model the following conversation and have students practice it in pairs. As a closing activity, provide a variety of objects for them to use as substitutions in the conversation.

Child 1:   *How many (eggs) do you have?*
Child 2:   *I have (one) (egg).*
            I have (two) (eggs).

Help students realize that the question requires a plural noun even if the answer is singular.

Using the Student Pages

Presenting the Story
Follow the suggestions in Presenting the Story Units, Lessons Two and Three (pages 11–14) for reading and discussing parts 1 and 2 of "Anansi."

Presenting the Practice Page
As a warm-up, model and practice the conversation for possessive adjectives in the Getting Ready to Read section of this story unit. Then, show students the illustrations on the practice page and model the conversations for each pair of characters.

Firefly: *The eggs are mine.*
Anansi: *No, they're not yours. The eggs are mine.*

Anansi: *The eggs are mine.*
Tiger: *No, they're not yours. The eggs are mine.*

Ten Tales for Teaching English © Good Year Books.

Encourage students to talk about what is happening and about how each character feels. Give each child a copy of the practice page. Help students read the directions at the top of the page. Then, have them practice the conversations with a partner.

As a closing activity, help students read the question at the bottom of the page. Encourage them to talk about what happened in the story and elicit as much new vocabulary as possible.

Presenting the Application Page

The application page focuses on counting, naming the numerals 1–8, and matching the numeral to the number word. As a warm-up, write the numerals on the chalkboard and have students practice saying them in order and out of order. Next, write the number words on the chalkboard, and help students read them and then match them to the numerals.

Show students the application page, and help them read the question and directions at the top of the page. Help them identify Anansi and the eggs, and have them tell what happened in the story. Have them count the eggs and identify the numerals and number words. Model how the page is to be completed and give each student a copy of the application page, a pair of scissors, and some glue. Have them work in pairs to complete the page. Leave a completed page available for the students to use as a guide. Have students take turns counting the eggs, using the illustration as a guide.

Focus students' attention on the questions at the bottom of the page. Help them read and answer each question. Have them answer the questions by writing the correct numeral on the line (8). Students who have acquired more English can write the numeral and number word.

Presenting the Evaluation Page

As a warm-up for the evaluation page, show students the illustrations, flashcards, and any other visual aids from the story. Encourage them to tell what happened in the story. For children who are already reading and writing in English, write key sentences on the chalkboard for them. Next, show them the illustration on this page. Have them identify Anansi. Give each student a copy of the evaluation page. Help them read the directions at the top. Model how to assemble the Anansi puppet and retell the story using the puppet. Help students understand that Anansi is telling the story.

After students have assembled their puppets, have them sit in a circle. Going around the room, have children take turns using their puppets to say something about the story or something that happened in the story. Write their responses on the chalkboard; as a closing activity, work as a class to sequence them in the correct order.

As part of your unit evaluation, ask students to complete the Now I Know page following the guidelines in Presenting the Story Units, Lesson Six (pages 15–16).

Additional Activities

What is Your Favorite Food?

Have children talk about Anansi and his favorite food. Ask them what they think the other characters' foods might be. Give each child a piece of drawing paper, and have students draw their favorite foods. If they are already writing and reading in English, have them label their pictures. As a closing activity, have them share their work with the class.

Do you want to be Anansi?

Ask students, "Do you want to be Anansi?" Help them explain their answers. Continue with the other characters in the same way. As a closing activity, give each student a piece of drawing paper, and have children draw their favorite characters. Have them share their work with the class, telling why they like this character.

Ten Tales for Teaching English © Good Year Books.

Spider Webs

Draw a spider web and make a copy for each child. Show students how to make a spider web with a glue stick, by gluing the yarn over the lines. When they are finished gluing their webs, have them draw or cut and paste a picture of a spider in the web. As a closing activity, encourage students to talk about the story and what happened to Anansi.

Whose Shoe Is This?

To illustrate the possessive adjectives *mine* and *yours,* have children sit in a circle and each take off one shoe. Mix up the shoes and put them in a pile in the center of the circle. Next, give each child a shoe (not theirs). Have them find the owner of their shoe by using the following conversation.

Child 1:   *Is this yours?*
Child 2:   *Yes, it's mine.*

Learn a Poem With Writing Option

Show children the picture of Anansi on page 111. Show them a picture of a spider web. Read the poem below aloud, then have students practice saying it with you. Have them illustrate the poem. If children are already reading and writing in English, write the poem on the chalkboard for them to practice reading. Have them copy and illustrate it. As a closing activity, ask volunteers to say and act out the poem.

Spider, Spider

Spider, spider on the ground.
I see the spider walk around.
I see the spider climb each day.
To make a web, it spins away.

Anansi and the Eggs, Part 1

I know a little spider. Anansi is his name.
He likes to play all kinds of tricks. He thinks it is a game.

He lives with all his friends like the tiger and the snake.
He likes to trick them when he can. His tricks are no mistake.

Anansi likes to eat a lot. He eats so many things.
"My favorite food is eggs, you know," this is what he sings.

Anansi goes to Firefly's house. He knocks and says, "Hello.
Do you have any eggs to eat?" Firefly says, "No."

Firefly says, "It's OK. We can find good eggs tonight.
We can look together. I can use my light."

Anansi and Firefly go out into the night.
Anansi calls out, "Firefly, it's dark. Turn on your light."

Firefly turns on his light, and Anansi says, "That's fine.
Firefly, I see an egg. It is not yours. It's mine."

Anansi gets a lot of eggs. Anansi says, "I'm done.
I like to look for eggs with you. This is a lot of fun."

Firefly says, "Anansi, I do not think that this is fun.
I shine my light. You take the eggs and you leave me none."

Firefly says, "I'm going home." Firefly says, "Good night."
Firefly flies away. Now there is no light.

Anansi walks and walks and walks. He cannot see a thing.
He carries all his eggs with him. Then he starts to sing.

"Wake up. Wake up. Wake up, my friends. Can anyone hear me?
I need a place to sleep tonight. It's dark. I cannot see."

Tell what you know.

1. What does Anansi the Spider do?
2. What does Firefly do?

Ten Tales for Teaching English © Good Year Books.

Anansi and the Eggs, Part 2

He walks. He stops. He is afraid. What does Anansi hear?
He calls out, "Who is there? Please do not come near."

He walks a little more and then Anansi says, "Oh no!
It's Tiger!" Anansi says, "I guess it's time to go!"

Tiger laughs, "Anansi, friend, please come and stay the night.
You have eggs that I can cook. And, yes, I have a light."

Anansi goes to Tiger's house. You know, he is so scared.
Tiger cooks the eggs and says, "I want them to be shared."

"These eggs are good," says Tiger. He eats each and every one.
Anansi sits and watches. The eggs are gone. There are none!

"I'm tired," says the tiger. "It's time to say, 'Good night.'"
He puts a lobster in the egg pot and then turns off the light.

Anansi says, "I'm hungry. I know what I can do.
Maybe there's an egg for me. Maybe there are two."

He puts his hand into the pot and jumps and says, "Oh, no!"
The lobster bites him on the hand and then it bites his toe.

Anansi wakes up Tiger. Anansi knows what to do.
He says, "Good-bye," and then he says, "Thank you."

Firefly flies away and now when Anansi comes to play,
Firefly says, "I cannot play. Come back another day."

Anansi sits alone right now. He has no eggs or friends.
That's all for now. This story's done. For now this is the end.

Tell what you know.

1. What does Anansi the Spider do?
2. What does Tiger do?

Ten Tales for Teaching English © Good Year Books.

Practice Page

Whose eggs are these? Tell a friend.

1

The eggs are mine.   No. They're not yours.
The eggs are mine.

2

The eggs are mine.   No. They're not yours.
The eggs are mine.

What happens to the eggs?

Application Page

How many? Cut and paste.

two

one

three

four

five

six

seven

eight

1   3   5   7

2   4   6   8

How many eggs does Anansi have? _____

How many legs does Anansi have? _____

Evaluation Page

Make a puppet. Help Anansi tell the story.

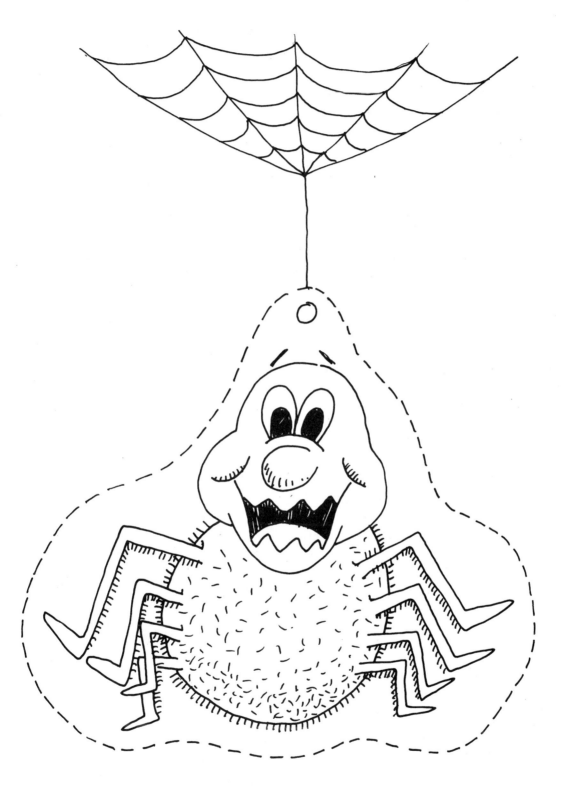

You will need some yarn.

Overview

Story Synopsis

A man works every day as a stonecutter. He is cutting stone from a mountain to make a new fountain for the king. One day, he wishes to be the king. The magic of the mountain grants his wish. He is now the king. As he stands in the sun, he gets very hot and realizes that the sun is stronger than he is. He now wishes to be the sun. The magic mountain grants his wish and makes him the sun. As the sun, he is very powerful, until a cloud covers him. Because he now thinks the cloud is more powerful, he wishes to be the cloud. As the cloud, he thinks he is very strong so he floods everything he sees. The mountain, however, does not flood. So, he wishes to be the mountain because he thinks that it is more powerful. As the mountain, he thinks he is the strongest until he hears the cling, cling of a stonecutter chipping away at him. He realizes that the stonecutter is stronger than the mountain and wishes to be the stonecutter again. After all this, he is finally happy. This story's origin can be traced to Asia. It has versions in Chinese and Japanese literature.

Unit Objectives

- to become familiar with the story

- to sequence events in a story

- to talk about wishes

- to use regular verbs and the verb *to be* in the simple present tense

- to use predicate adjectives

- to use comparative adjectives

- to answer questions with *who, what,* and *how* in the simple present tense

- to act out the story

- to talk about the weather

Ten Tales for Teaching English © Good Year Books.

Getting Ready to Read

Warm-Up

Bring in a hammer and a stone and play the following "Look" game with students. Put the hammer and stone in a bag and have students take turns putting their hands in the bag and trying to guess what the items are without looking. After every student has had a turn, help them identify the hammer and stone. Then show them the illustration on page 123. Ask volunteers to tell what they see and what is happening in the pictures. Ask students if they know a story that goes with this picture. Allow volunteers to share details about the story of "The Stonecutter." If students are not familiar with the story, offer some details from the synopsis and encourage students to guess what happens to the man at the end of the story. Students with limited conversation skills can draw pictures to show what they think will happen.

Vocabulary and Grammar Preview

Verbs	Nouns	Adjectives	Other
cut	cling cling	strong	cloudy
hammer	*cloud	stronger	rainy
sing	flood		snowy
wish	fountain		sunny
work	hammer		windy
	job		
	*king		
	*mountain		
	*rain		
	stone		
	stonecutter		
	*sun		

Grammatical Structures: simple present tense, predicate adjectives, comparative adjectives

Decide which words and structures are new and which are review for your students. Follow the suggestions in Presenting the Story Units, Lesson One (pages 8–11) for appropriate vocabulary and grammar activities. Note that flashcards for the starred words are available on pages 156–164.

Because the verb *wish* can be an abstract concept for young children, you might want to introduce it by showing the children the illustration from the story "The Wishes" on page 135 and the fairy in the story "Cinderella." Hold up a visual aid such as a picture of some ice cream and say, "I do not have any ice cream. I wish for some ice cream." Pretend the fairy from the story grants your wish. Hold up another illustration of something desirable (maybe a picture of a puppy) and invite volunteers to come up and make a wish about it. Help them follow the model you presented. Give each student a piece of drawing paper. Have them illustrate their individual wishes. As a closing activity, have students share their wishes with the class using the model provided, "I wish for a (puppy)." Since children may draw something they do not know how to say in English, model vocabulary when necessary. Depending on children's ability levels, this lesson might take thirty minutes to present. Be prepared to use one extra class period.

This story unit presents the comparative form of the adjective *strong/stronger.* Act out the adjective *strong* for students and model the sentence *I am strong.* by holding up a (heavy stone). Have a student come up and act out the adjective *strong* doing the same thing. Next, show students a pile of heavier stones. Pick them up and say, "I am stronger than (Bob)." Illustrate other adjectives such as *tall/taller* and *small/smaller.* Help students use the correct form by adding the final *-er* to the adjective plus *than.*

Students who have acquired more English can use substitutions for this form such as *tall/taller, small/smaller, big/bigger, thin/thinner, fat/fatter, hot/hotter, cold/colder.*

Write the adjectives in two columns on the chalkboard to show the contrast between the spellings. Help students read the words and use them in sentences. As a closing activity, line up students in size order and generate sentences about them using the adjectives *taller* and *smaller*. Use the following model conversation.

Child 1: *I am (taller) than (Greg).*
Child 2: *I am (smaller) than (Alex).*

The application page (see page 125) presents weather words as new vocabulary. Use the suggestions in the section, Presenting the Application Page on page 116, when presenting this new vocabulary. Model the following conversation for students, and have them practice it with you. After they are familiar with it, have them work in pairs and then present their conversations for the rest of the class. Use the corresponding "weather word" flashcards at the end of the book as prompts.

Child 1: *What is the weather like today?*
Child 2: *It's (rainy).*

Some substitutions are *rainy, sunny, windy, cloudy, snowy.*

Using the Student Pages

Presenting the Story
Follow the suggestions in Presenting the Story Units, Lessons Two and Three (pages 11–14) for reading and discussing parts 1 and 2 of "The Stonecutter."

Presenting the Practice Page
As a warm-up, show students the illustrations from the story, and have them tell you what happened. Encourage them to talk about the wishes that the stonecutter made. Next, show them the illustrations on the practice page (see page 124). Have them identify the characters and to tell what happened in the correct order. Write students' answers on the chalkboard for them.

Give each student a copy of the practice page. Help them read the directions at the top of the page. Model the question and answers for each pair of illustrations. Have students practice the question and answers with you. After they are familiar with the conversation, have them work in pairs asking and answering the question using the model provided. Ask volunteers to act out the conversation, using the illustrations as prompts. Students who are already reading and writing in English can write a sentence about each picture on a separate piece of paper. Provide and model any necessary written vocabulary for students.

Who is stronger?
1. The sun is stronger than the king.
2. The cloud is stronger than the sun.
3. The mountain is stronger than the cloud.
4. The stonecutter is stronger than the mountain.

As a closing activity, focus students' attention on the question at the bottom of the page. Have them talk about who they would like to be and why. Give each child a piece of drawing paper and have children draw a picture of who they want to be in the story. Have them share their work with the class. Students who are already writing in English can write one or two sentences about their pictures.

Presenting the Application Page

The application page focuses on describing the weather and using weather words. If these words are new to your students, use the illustrations and flashcards to present the new vocabulary. See the section, Presenting the Story Units, for suggestions and activities.

As a warm-up, ask children, "What's the weather like today?" Have them look out the window and model the following sentence: It's (sunny) today. Ask volunteers to add more adjectives. Write their responses on the chalkboard. Show students the flashcards for the weather illustrations on the application page. Model the conversation and new words for students.

Teacher: *What's the weather like?*
Children: *It's (windy, cloudy, rainy, sunny, snowy).*

After students are familiar with the vocabulary and conversation pattern, show them how to assemble the weather wheel and spinner. Give each child a copy of the application page. Help them read the directions at the top of the page. Direct children to color the weather wheel first, then assemble it.

Have students work in groups or pairs, taking turns spinning and talking about the weather. Have them use the conversation model. If time is an issue, or you are working with kindergarten children who might have trouble cutting and assembling, prepare one spinner for each group, and have children take turns spinning and talking about the weather.

As a closing activity, have students talk about the weather words and how they relate to the story "The Stonecutter."

Presenting the Evaluation Page

As a warm-up for the evaluation page, show students the illustrations, flashcards, and any other visual aids from the story. Encourage them to tell what happened in the correct order. For children who are already reading and writing in English, write key sentences on the chalkboard for them. Next, show them the illustrations on this page. Have them tell what is happening in each picture and help them sequence the pictures correctly. Give each student a copy of the evaluation page. Help them read the directions at the top. Model how to follow the directions, and then have students complete the page independently.

As a closing activity, have children retell the story for a friend or the class using the illustrations on this page. Have students who are already writing in English write one or two sentences about each picture on a separate piece of paper.

As part of your unit evaluation, ask students to complete the Now I Know page following the guidelines in Presenting the Story Units, Lesson Six (pages 15–16).

Additional Activities

Act It Out

As a warm up, show students the illustrations, flashcards, and any other visual aids from the story. Encourage students to tell what happened in the story. Write key sentences on the chalkboard for them. Help students sequence the sentences so they are in the correct order. Use the illustrations on the evaluation page to make puppets. Paste them on paper bags or attach them to craft sticks, and read the following puppet play while you act out the story.

The Stonecutter:	*I wish and I wish. I want to be the king.*
The Magic Mountain:	*You are the king.*
The King:	*I wish and I wish. The sun is stronger than I am. I want to be the sun.*
The Magic Mountain:	*You are the sun.*
The Sun:	*I wish and I wish. The cloud is stronger than I am. I want to be the cloud.*
The Magic Mountain:	*You are the cloud.*
The Cloud:	*I wish and I wish. The mountain is stronger than I am. I want to be the mountain.*
The Magic Mountain:	*You are the mountain.*
A Stonecutter:	*Cling, Cling, Cling.*
The Mountain:	*The stonecutter is stronger than I am. I want to be a stonecutter.*
The Magic Mountain:	*You are a stonecutter.*
The Stonecutter:	*Now I am happy.*

As a closing activity, encourage students to tell the story in their own words.

Who Do You Want to Be?

As a warm up, show students the illustrations, flashcards, and any other visual aids from the story. Encourage them to tell what happened in the story, and write key sentences on the chalkboard for them. Show students the illustrations on the evaluation page, and have them talk about their favorite characters using the following model:

Teacher:	*Who do you want to be?*
Child:	*I want to be the (sun).*
Teacher:	*Why do you want to be the sun?*
Child:	*The sun is stronger than the king.*

Help students talk about the stonecutter and why he is happy at the end of the story.

As a closing activity, have students cut out their favorite characters from this page and paste them on separate pieces of paper. Help them write two sentences about the picture using this model: *I want to be the (sun). The (sun) is stronger than the (king).*

What's The Weather Like Today?

As a warm-up, review weather vocabulary using the weather wheel on the application page. Talk about what the weather is like "today." Give each child a piece of drawing paper and have students draw a picture of today's weather. Children who are already reading and writing in English can either label or write a sentence about their pictures.

Keep a Weather Calendar

Draw a large calendar on tag board or heavy paper. Label it with the current month and fill in the days of the week and numbers for each day. Leave enough room for children to draw pictures illustrating the weather for each day. As a daily warm-up, discuss the weather and have children take turns drawing the pictures to show what the weather is like for each day of the month.

Write About It

Write the following word list and sentences on the chalkboard. Help children read and complete the sentences with the correct rhyming words. As a closing activity, ask volunteers to take turns reading the completed sentences.

mountain	cloud	king	sun

1. I wish and I wish and I sing and I sing.
   I don't want to cut stone. I want to be _____.

2. I wish and I wish and I think I am done.
   I don't want to be king. I want to be the _____.

3. I wish and I wish and I sing very loud.
   I don't want to be the sun I want to be a _____.

4. A man hammers and cuts to make stone from the _____.
   He works very hard to make the king a new fountain.

Ten Tales for Teaching English © Good Year Books.

The Stonecutter, Part 1

A man cuts and he hammers to make stone for the king.
He works and he works and he always sings,

"This is my job, to cut stone from the mountain.
The king needs the stone to make a new fountain."

One day the man says, "I am tired of this.
I don't want to cut stone. I want to make a wish."

"I wish and I wish and I sing and I sing.
I don't want to cut stone. I want to be king."

The mountain is magic. He hears the man sing.
The mountain says, "Man, now you are king."

The man looks around and what does he see?
He sees that he's king and dressed beautifully!

The king says, "I am hot," and asks himself, "Why?"
"Here's the answer," he says, "the sun is stronger than I."

The man says, "Now I am tired of this.
I don't want to be king. I want to make a wish."

"I wish and I wish and I sing and I sing.
I want to be the sun. I don't want to be king."

The mountain is magic. He hears the man sing.
The mountain says, "You are the sun, not a king."

Tell what you know.

1. What happens to the man?

2. What are the man's wishes?

Ten Tales for Teaching English © Good Year Books.

The Stonecutter, Part 2

The sun is so strong. He burns all the trees.
He burns all the flowers and all that he sees.

The sun says, "I'm covered." He asks himself, "Why?"
"Look. There's a cloud. The cloud's stronger than I."

"I wish and I wish and I sing and I sing.
I want to be a cloud, not the sun, not the king."

The mountain is magic. He hears the man sing.
"You are a cloud, not the sun, not the king."

The cloud is strong and says, "Look at me.
I rain on the flowers and all of the trees."

The cloud says, "But, the mountain's not covered. Oh, why?"
The cloud says, "The mountain is stronger than I."

"I wish and I wish and I sing very loud.
I want to be a mountain, not a cloud."

The mountain is magic and asks, "Are you done?
You are the mountain, not a cloud, not the sun."

The mountain hears a "cling cling" and asks, "Why?
The answer is something is stronger than I."

A man cuts and cuts to make stone from the mountain,
He hammers to make stone for the king's new fountain.

The mountain says, "I wish to cut stone in the sun.
Please, magic mountain, my wishes are done."

The mountain is magic, and says, "You are done.
You are the stonecutter, not a cloud, not the sun."

The stonecutter hammers to make stone for the king.
He works and he works and he always sings,

"This is my job and I know that I can
Be happy each day just being a man."

Tell what you know.

1. What happens to the man?

2. Who does the man want to be?

Practice Page

Who is stronger? Tell a friend.

Who do you want to be? Draw a picture.

Ten Tales for Teaching English © Good Year Books.

Application Page

What is the weather like? Cut. Make a weather wheel.

You will need one of these.

Evaluation Page
Cut. Paste. Tell the story.

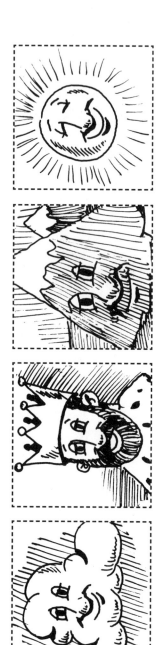

Ten Tales for Teaching English © Good Year Books.

OverView

Story Synopsis

One day, as a man is walking in the woods, he meets a fairy. The fairy gives the man three wishes and tells him to use them wisely. The man runs home to his wife to tell her the good news. He is so happy and excited that he gives her one of his wishes. The man sits down to eat dinner and the woman places soup before him. The man wishes for meat instead. The man's wife becomes very angry because he has wasted a wish. The man, in turn, becomes angry with his wife and wishes for the meat to be on her nose. The woman is very upset and asks the man to use his last wish to help her. He wishes for the meat to be back on the dish and has no more wishes. In the end, they realize how foolish they were and that they do not want any more wishes, just a good day. This folk tale is by the Grimm Brothers but has origins in Hungary. A similar tale exists in the literature of Puerto Rico.

Unit Objectives

- to become familiar with the story

- to sequence events in a story

- to talk about different kinds of food

- to tell what one wants to eat

- to tell what one has

- to talk about wishes and to understand what a wish is

- to use regular verbs and the verb *to be* in the simple present tense

- to use predicate adjectives

- to answer questions with *who, what,* and *how* in the simple present tense

- to use singular and plural nouns

- to use *some* for mass and plural nouns

- to use mass nouns

Getting Ready to Read

Warm-Up

Show pictures of bread, cheese, juice, meat, milk, and soup. Help students identify these foods and tell what they like to eat. Next, show children the illustration on page 136 and invite them to talk about the picture. Have them identify the food that they see and tell you what is funny in this picture. Encourage students to guess how the meat got on the woman's nose. Ask students if they know a story that goes with this picture. Allow volunteers to share details about the story of "The Wishes." If students are not familiar with the story, offer some details from the synopsis and encourage students to guess how the characters get the meat off the woman's nose. Students with limited conversation skills can draw pictures to show what they think will happen.

Vocabulary and Grammar Preview

Verbs	Nouns	Adjectives	Other
drink	*bread	angry	some
eat	*carrots	great	
have	cheese	sorry	
see	dish		
walk	*fairy		
wish	juice		
	man		
	*meat		
	*milk		
	*nose		
	*pan		
	*pears		
	soda (pop)		
	soup		
	water		
	wife		
	wish		

Grammatical Structures: simple present tense, predicate adjectives, singular and plural nouns, count nouns, *some* with mass/plural nouns

Ten Tales for Teaching English © Good Year Books.

Decide which words and structures are new and which are review for your students. Follow the suggestions in Presenting the Story Units, Lesson One (pages 8–11) for appropriate vocabulary and grammar activities. Note that flashcards for the starred words are available on pages 156–164.

The verb *wish* can be an abstract concept for young children. See page 114 in the story unit "The Stonecutter" for suggestions on presenting this verb.

Act out the predicate adjectives for students. After you have modeled these words, and children have practiced them, have students act them out as you say them. Reverse roles, and have the children say the words as you act them out.

Use the following conversation and vocabulary with students to practice using *some* with mass/plural nouns. Model the conversation and, after students are familiar with it, have them repeat it after you. Have children work in pairs and take turns being Child 1 and Child 2.

Child 1:   *What do you want to eat/drink?*
Child 2:   *I want some (juice).*

This conversation works well with the vocabulary and illustrations on the application page.

As a contrast, use count nouns in the conversation and have students use the articles *a* and/or *the* when answering. Help them understand that *the* and *a* are used when talking about only one item. The flashcards at the back of this book for the following singular noun food words may be helpful: *bun, pear, plum, peach.*

Finally, use plural nouns in the conversation and have students use the adjective *some* when answering. There are flashcards at the back of this book for the following plural noun food words: *eggs, peppers, carrots, potatoes.*

SUM

Using the Student Pages

Presenting the Story

Follow the suggestions in Presenting the Story Units, Lessons Two and Three (pages 11–14) for reading and discussing parts 1 and 2 of "The Wishes."

Presenting the Practice Page

As a warm-up, review the story using the illustrations and any other visual aids. Encourage students to tell what happened in the story, and write key sentences on the chalkboard. Help students sequence the sentences so they are in the correct order. Show students the story wheel on the practice page, and have them tell what is happening in each picture. Help students read the directions at the top of the page. Model how to put the story wheel together and how it works. Spin the spinner and describe story events using the simple present tense and the adjective *some* when talking about the food items.

> *He walks in the woods.*
> *He has some meat.*
> *They have some soup.*
> *The meat is on her nose.*

Give each child a story wheel and a butterfly clip, and have them work in pairs or groups to assemble it. Have students take turns spinning the story wheel and telling what happens in each picture. Children who have acquired more English can describe what is going to happen next or what happened first. As a closing activity, have students talk about the characters and their wishes. Give students the opportunity to tell what they would have wished for. Have them role play the story. Say, "You are the man/woman. You have three wishes. What do you want?"

Presenting the Application Page

As a warm-up, show students visual aids for bread, juice, meat, milk, soda, and soup. Have them practice this vocabulary using the conversation on the next page.

Ten Tales for Teaching English © Good Year Books.

Child 1: *What do you want to eat?*
Child 2: *I want some (bread).*
Child 1: *What do you want to drink?*
Child 2: *I want some (soda).*

Ask students to pick their favorite foods from the list and tell a partner.

Child 1: *What is your favorite food?*
Child 2: *My favorite food is (bread).*

Point out to students that the article *some* is not used in the second part of this conversation.

Show students the application page. Have them identify the pictures and decide what they want to eat. Help them read the directions at the top of the page. Model how to complete the page.

> *"I want some (carrots)."*
> *(Paste the picture of carrots in a box.)*

Give students a copy of this page, scissors, and glue. Have them work in pairs to complete the page, pasting in two food choices and one drink choice. Have them work in groups or pairs using the conversation above. As a closing activity, invite students to tell the class what they want to eat and drink. Students who are already reading and writing in English can write a sentence for each of their choices.

Presenting the Evaluation Page

As a warm-up for the evaluation page, show students the illustrations, flashcards, and any other visual aids from the story. Encourage them to tell what happened in the correct order. For children who are already reading and writing in English, write key sentences on the chalkboard for them. Next, show students the illustrations on this page. Have students tell what is happening in each picture. Help them realize that the pictures are out of order. Read the directions aloud. Model how to follow the directions. Then, have students complete the page independently.

As a closing activity, have children retell the story for a friend or the class using the illustrations on the evaluation page. Have students who are already writing in English write one or two sentences about each picture on a separate piece of paper.

As part of your unit evaluation, ask students to complete the Now I Know page following the guidelines in Presenting the Story Units, Lesson Six (pages 15–16).

Additional Activities

Classifying Wishes

As a warm-up, review what happened in the story and focus on the wishes that the man made. Help students decide if the wishes were good or bad—wise or unwise—wishes. Give each child a piece of drawing paper and have them draw and label two columns: *A Wise Wish* and *An Unwise Wish.* Have students draw the wishes in the story or draw what they consider wise and unwise wishes. Students who are already writing in English can write one or two sentences about their pictures. As a closing activity, ask volunteers to share their work with the rest of the class.

Learn a Poem: Star Light, Star Bright

Review the story with students and focus on the wishes the man made. Write the following poem on the chalkboard, and help students read and talk about wishes they would like to make. Teach the poem by modeling it and having children repeat it after you, line by line. When they are familiar with the poem, have students copy it on a piece of writing paper and illustrate the wish they would like to make. As a closing activity, invite students to say the poem and talk about their pictures.

Star Light, Star Bright

Star Light, Star Bright,
First star I see tonight,
I wish I could, I wish I might,
Have the wish I wish tonight.

Act It Out: In a Restaurant

As a warm-up, review food items and any other vocabulary students have learned that fit a conversation about ordering food in a restaurant. Model the conversation and have students practice it with you. Have them take turns acting out the dialogue, playing the parts of the waiter/waitress and the customer. Encourage students who are already writing in English to write the food order on a piece of paper. Monitor students' use of the adjective *some*.

Waiter/Waitress:	*What do you want to eat?*
Customer:	*I want some (meat).*
Waiter/Waitress:	*What do you want to drink?*
Customer:	*I want some (milk).*

Have the waiter/waitress tell the rest of the class what the customer wants.

He/She wants some (milk) and some (meat).

As a closing activity, have students talk about going to a restaurant and what they would like to order.

Puppet Play

Use the various illustrations in the unit to make puppets by either pasting the pictures on paper bags or attaching them to craft sticks. As a warm-up, show students the illustrations, flashcards, and any other visual aids from the story. Encourage them to tell what happened in the story, and write key sentences on the chalkboard for them. Help children sequence the sentences so they are in the correct order. Give students copies of the illustrations from the unit, glue, and paper bags or craft sticks. Model how to assemble a puppet, and have students work in groups. Read the following puppet play while you act out the story. Help children practice it with you and, when they are familiar with it, assign the parts of the characters. Have students work in groups to practice their roles. Then, have each group put on their puppet play for the rest of the class. Give students who are already reading in English a copy of the play and have them read their parts.

Fairy: *I am the fairy. Please sit with me.*
Here are your wishes, one, two, three.

Man: *I have three wishes. I know what to do.*
Here, my wife, I give one to you.

Woman: *Thank you so much. Now please take a seat.*
Here is some soup. It's time to eat.

Man: *No, thank you. I want some meat.*
I wish for some meat that I can eat.

Woman: *Now I am angry. Now you only have two,*
One wish for me and one wish for you!

Man: *Now I am angry, I am angry like you,*
I can make wishes. I know what to do!
I wish for the meat on that very small dish
to be on your nose. That is my wish!

Woman: *Oh no! Take this meat off my nose. Make a wish.*
Please wish for the meat to be on the dish.

Man: *I'm sorry, I'm sorry. Oh well, here goes,*
I wish for the meat to be off your small nose.

Man and Woman:

Thank you. Oh, thank you. Do you know what we say?
We do not want wishes. We just want a good day.

Ten Tales for Teaching English © Good Year Books.

The Wishes, Part 1

A man in the woods walks. What does he see?
He sees a fairy. She says, "Please, sit with me."

"I give you three wishes. Use them wisely, now.
Good-by," says the fairy. The man says, "Oh, wow!"

He runs to his wife. He knows what to do.
He says, "I have three wishes. Here's one for you."

"A wish just for me," says his wife. "This is great!
Here is your dinner and you are late!"

His wife smiles and says, "Here's soup. Now, please eat."
He says, "I don't want soup. I wish for some meat."

"Look, the meat's on the dish," says the man.
His wife is surprised. She drops her small pan!

His wife is so angry. "Now we have two,
One wish for me and one wish for you."

Tell what you know.

1. How many wishes does the man have?
2. What does the man wish for?

The Wishes, Part 2

The man says, "These wishes are mine, none for you."
The man is so angry. What does he do?

He says, "I wish for this meat on the dish,
To be on your nose. Yes, that is my wish!"

The man looks and says, "Look at you now!
The meat's on your nose! Oh, no! Oh, wow!"

"Take this meat off my nose," says his wife. "Make a wish.
Wish for the meat to be on that small dish!"

The man looks and says, "Oh my! Well, here goes!
I wish for the meat to be off your small nose."

His wife says, "I'm sorry." The man's sorry, too.
They have no more wishes. Do you know what they do?

They sit. They eat soup. Do you know what they say?
"We do not want wishes. We just want a good day."

Tell what you know.

1. What does the man wish for?
2. Do they want more wishes?

Ten Tales for Teaching English © Good Year Books.

Practice Page

Cut. Make a story wheel. Tell the story. Act it out.

You will need one of these.

Application Page

Name each food. What do you want to eat? What do you want to drink?
Cut and paste. Tell a friend.

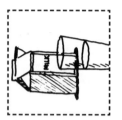

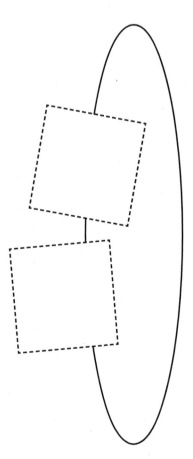

Ten Tales for Teaching English © Good Year Books.

Evaluation Page

Cut and paste. Do this story puzzle. Tell what happens.

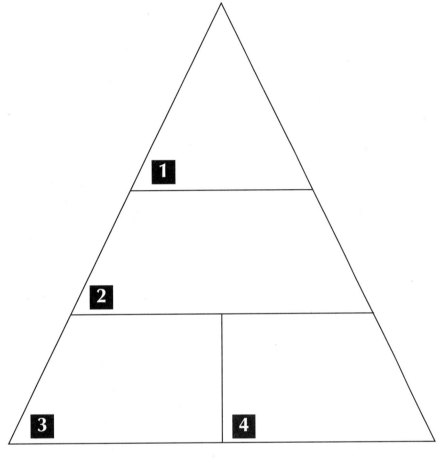

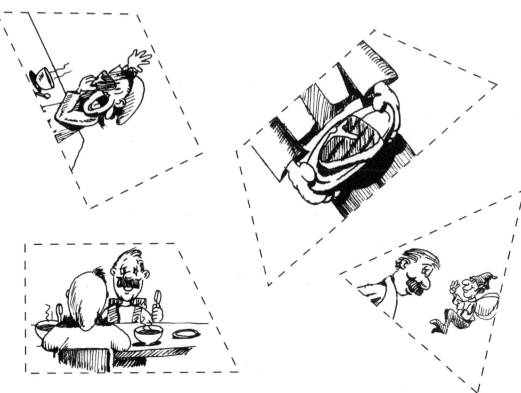

Overview

Story Synopsis

Paul Bunyon was born in Maine, U.S.A. The legend says that he was a giant. In this version, he is as tall as a mountain, has legs as long as very long trees, and a thumb as large as a big fish. Paul Bunyon is best known as a lumberman with a big, blue ox named Babe. Paul and Babe needed more room so they moved to Alaska, U.S.A., where there was more space to play. At the end of the story, it is suggested that, if you ever meet them, you should introduce yourself by saying, "How do you do?" Stories of giants can be found in the literature of many different cultures. The story of Paul Bunyon comes from the United States.

Unit Objectives

- to become familiar with the story

- to talk about where one lives and where one is from

- to talk about the difference between legends and reality

- to use regular verbs and the verb *to be* in the simple present tense

- to use adjectives

- to answer questions with *who, what,* and *how* in the simple present tense

- to use singular and plural nouns

- to use similes

- to identify body parts and play bingo

- to use a map of the United States

- to name and identify the colors, *blue, green, orange, red*

Getting Ready to Read

Warm-Up

Play Simon Says with students by naming body parts and having children point to those parts only when you say "Simon Says." Then, write or place visual aids for the vocabulary on the chalkboard or chalkboard ledge for students to use as a reference. Draw a picture of a giant man by including a tree or a house in your drawing that looks much smaller than the man. Have students talk about the size of the giant's arms, legs, eyes, and so on. If time permits, provide students with a very large piece of paper or oak tag and, as a group, draw a picture of a giant.

Then, show students the illustrations on pages 150 and 151. Ask volunteers to tell what they see in the pictures, and have them describe the sizes of what they see. Ask students if they know a story that goes with this picture. Allow volunteers to share details about the story of Paul Bunyon. If students are not familiar with the story, offer some details from the synopsis and encourage students to guess how big Paul Bunyon is and what he does. Students with limited conversation skills can draw pictures to show what they think will happen.

Vocabulary and Grammar Preview

Verbs	Nouns	Adjectives	Other
plant	ax	big	blue
play	*broccoli	hungry	green
run	*carrots	loud	orange
rumble	cup	tall	red
tumble	*cloud		*arms
	dish		*eyes
	door		*feet
	*fish		*hands
	game		*head
	gate		*knees
	*giant		*leg
	*meat		*toe
	map		thumb
	*milk		Alaska
	*ox		Maine
	*potatoes		U.S.A.
	table		
	*tree		
	wheel		

Grammatical Structures: simple present tense, similes, adjectives, singular and plural nouns

Decide which words and structures are new and which are review for your students. Follow the suggestions in Presenting the Story Units, Lesson One (pages 8–11) for appropriate vocabulary and grammar activities. Note that flashcards for the starred words are available on pages 156–164.

When presenting body parts, use the suggestions for presenting nouns given in the section, Presenting the Story Units. Use the pictures from the bingo game on the evaluation page of this unit and the pictures on

Ten Tales for Teaching English © Good Year Books.

the practice page on page 152 as your visual aids when presenting or reviewing this vocabulary. Check students' comprehension of this vocabulary through the following Total Physical Response techniques. As you say a body part, have students respond by touching the corresponding part on their own body. After they are familiar with the game, say the body parts in groups of two or three, and have students touch those parts of their bodies in the correct order.

The unit presents body part names in both the singular and plural forms. Use the suggestion given in the section, Presenting the Story Units, when working with these words.

The application page on page 153 focuses on map skills and working with the states of Alaska, Maine, and the state where your class lives. Mark these locations on a separate copy of the application page before you begin your lesson. This will allow students to easily see which states you are talking about. Students should not be responsible for naming all of the states, unless it is something that is being taught in the ESL curriculum or mainstream classroom. Use the map as an introduction to map skills and as an introduction to social studies of the United States.

This story unit also presents similes. It is important for children to understand that the two nouns in a simile have a relationship that is governed by the adjective. (Note: students will be working with similes that contain nouns.) If children are in a more advanced ESL class, they can make up their own similes about Paul Bunyon and Babe the Ox. Help students understand that the characters are fictional and that the similes illustrate a character larger than anyone could be in real life.

If children are already reading and writing in English, have them create a fable-like character and write similes describing it. (See Additional Activities on page 148.) Help students use the similes in the story by showing the corresponding visual aids. Model the similes and practice them with students. After they are familiar with the conversation, have them work in pairs to practice it. As a closing activity, invite students to tell how big Paul Bunyon is, along with other items in the story, using similes.

Child 1:   *How (tall) is (Paul Bunyon)?*
Child 2:   *Paul is as (tall) as a (mountain).*

Suggestions for substitutions include:

> *Paul Bunyon is as wide as a mountain.*
> *His eyes are as big as a very large dish*
> *His thumb is as big as a very large fish.*
> *His legs are as long as two very tall trees.*
> *His plate is as big as a door (table or gate).*
> *Babe is as big as a train.*
> *Paul's cup is as big as a wheel.*

Students who have acquired more English can provide similes for the nouns *knees, head, toe.*

Use the suggestions given in Presenting the Story Units to present the adjectives (see page 11). If students are unfamiliar with the color words *green, red, orange,* and *blue,* present them by using a variety of visual aids, such as crayons, markers, colored pencils, and so on. Help students ask and answer questions using the following patterns.

Child 1:   *What color is it?*
Child 2:   *It is (red).*
Child 1:   *What color is the (pencil)?*
Child 2:   *The (pencil) is (red).*

If children are unfamiliar with the verb *live,* show them a picture of a house or apartment building. Use familiar vocabulary and lexical frames such as, *I live in a house. I live in an apartment. I live here.* Encourage children to talk about where they live. Model the following conversation and have them practice it in pairs. As a closing activity, encourage students to tell the class where they live.

Child 1:   *Where do you live?*
Child 2:   *I live in (California).*

Ten Tales for Teaching English © Good Year Books.

Help students tell where they are from by first showing a globe or map of the world. Help students find and talk about their native countries. Model the following conversation and have students practice it with you. Invite them to take both parts, asking and telling where they are from.

Child 1:   *Where are you from?*
Child 2:   *I am from (Honduras).*

Using the Student Pages

Presenting the Story

Follow the suggestions in Presenting the Story Units, Lessons Two and Three (pages 11–14) for reading and discussing parts 1 and 2 of "Paul Bunyon."

Presenting the Practice Page

As a warm-up, play a quick game of Simon Says to review the body parts vocabulary. Help students use the correct forms for singular and plural nouns. (See Presenting the Story Units, pages 10–11, for suggestions on presenting these nouns.) Encourage students to talk about Paul Bunyon and use similes to describe his thumb, legs, eyes, and so on. Use the model provided in the Grammar/Vocabulary Review for this unit.

Give each student a copy of the practice page. Help them read the directions at the top. First, show students an assembled puppet. Then, show them how to assemble the puppet. Provide each child with five butterfly clips and scissors. Have them work in pairs or groups to complete this activity.

After their puppets are finished, have them practice the model dialogue in the Grammar/Vocabulary Review for this unit, taking turns asking and answering about Paul Bunyon's physical attributes. As a closing activity, invite students to come up and talk about Paul Bunyon using the similes they have practiced. More advanced students can provide similes of their own.

Presenting the Application Page

The application page is an introduction to map skills using a map of the United States. As a warm-up, show students a map of the United States, and help children locate and name the state where they are living. Encourage them to use the model dialogue found in the Grammar/ Vocabulary Review for this unit. Help students talk about the story. Help them tell where Paul and Babe are from and where they live now. Locate the two states, Maine and Alaska, on the map and have students talk about Paul Bunyon and Babe using the following dialogue.

Child 1:   *Where is (Paul Bunyon) from?*
Child 2:   *(Paul Bunyon) is from Maine.*

Child 1:   *Where does (Paul Bunyon) live?*
Child 2:   *Paul Bunyon lives in (Alaska).*

Show students a copy of the application page. Help them talk about the pictures, telling where Paul Bunyon and Babe are from and where they live. Model the following conversation and have them practice it with you, asking and telling where they live.

Child 1:   *Where do you live?*
Child 2:   *I live in (Florida).*

Help students read the directions at the top of the page. Then model how to complete the page. Have children do the activity with you, in pairs or groups. Show children the state on the map where they live, and have them color this state green. Help them fill in the name of their state on the line. For kindergarten students, fill in the state for them and have them answer the question as you read it to them. After students have completed the page, invite them to locate the three states. Say, "Show me (Alaska)."

Ten Tales for Teaching English © Good Year Books.

As a closing activity, help students read the last question on the page. Model the conversation and have them practice it with you. Have students practice the conversation in groups and then invite volunteers to come up and act out the conversation for the class.

Child 1:   *Where are you from?*
Child 2:   *I am from (Poland).*

Presenting the Evaluation Page

As a warm-up for the evaluation page, show students the illustrations, flashcards, and any other visual aids from the story. Use the puppet on the practice page to review the names of the body parts using the correct singular and plural forms for these nouns. Have students describe Paul Bunyon and Babe the Blue Ox using similes. Have students tell where they are from and where they live. For children who are already reading and writing in English, write key sentences on the chalkboard for them. Next, show students the illustrations on the evaluation page. Have them name the body parts using the correct singular and plural forms for these words. Show students how to paste the pictures in the boxes to make their "bingo boards." Give each student nine markers (such as paper clips). Explain how the game is played. Use a set of flashcards for the body parts, and mix them up like a deck of cards. Choose the top card, and have students provide a complete sentence: *This is the head, These are the feet,* and so on. As you say each body part, place your "marker" on the picture. Show students how they can win by placing markers on three squares in a row in any direction. Students must name their winning row in order to get credit for the win. The player who wins can be the "caller" for the next game.

As a closing activity, have children talk about the body part names on the evaluation page and relate them to the story of Paul Bunyon using similes.

As part of your unit evaluation, ask students to complete the Now I Know page following the guidelines in Presenting the Story Units, Lesson Six (pages 15–16).

Additional Activities

Measure Up

Have children line up in height order at the front of the classroom. Help them find someone in the class who is about their same height. Have students work in pairs to measure each other and record their heights on a piece of paper. Transfer this information onto the chalkboard, providing names and heights in inches. Help students generate similes about the class using the height measurements:

> *Greg is as tall as Alex.*

All About Me

Give each child a piece of brown wrapping paper large enough to draw full-size pictures of themselves. Have them work in pairs and take turns tracing each other onto the brown paper. Have students color their pictures, drawing the face and coloring the hair. When they are finished, ask volunteers to talk about themselves, using their pictures as prompts. Students can also work in pairs and record the lengths of their arms and legs. Transfer this information onto the chalkboard, and have students tell whose arms/legs are the same size using similes:

> *Bob's legs are as long as Joe's legs.*

Display students' pictures in the class or hallway for everyone to share and admire.

Fact vs. Fiction

As a warm-up, use the illustrations and visual aids from the story to talk about Paul Bunyon's physical attributes in the form of similes. Explain that he is a fictional character based on a legend and that he really doesn't exist. Ask students if they know of any other characters that are similar to Paul Bunyon, and have them use similes to describe them. Help children develop their own class fictional character. Have them name their character and describe it using similes. Help students develop and write stories about their new character. Have them illustrate the character and story, and then ask volunteers to share their work with the class. This activity will probably require more than one class period—one to develop the character and one to develop, write, and illustrate the story. Write the following prompts on the chalkboard to help children develop their stories.

Our Own Legend

Name:

He is as _____.

Things he does

What happens to (him)

How the story ends

Paul Bunyon, Part 1

There is a great man, his first name is Paul,
His last name is Bunyon. He is very tall.

He is so very tall, that sometimes, you know,
You can't see his head, just his big toe!

A giant we call him, so big and so tall,
As tall as a mountain, as wide as a wall.

His eyes are as big as a very large dish!
His thumb is as big as a very large fish!

His legs are as long as two very tall trees.
When I look up at him, I see two very big knees!

Paul Bunyon does many things, you know.
He cuts trees with his ax and helps new ones grow.

When he cuts down a tree, he plants a new one, you see,
So there will always be trees for you and for me.

When he is hungry, do you know what he eats?
He eats potatoes and carrots and broccoli and meat!

He eats so much food that the size of his plate,
is as big as a door or a table or a gate!

He needs forty cooks to make just one meal.
He drinks from a cup that's as big as a wheel.

Tell what you know.

1. How big is Paul Bunyon?
2. What does Paul Bunyon do?

Ten Tales for Teaching English © Good Year Books.

Paul Bunyon, Part 2

Paul has an ox that's as big as a train.
This ox is blue and Babe is his name.

They wrestle and roll in the dirt. They are loud.
They make such a mess, the dirt looks like a cloud!

Paul and Babe, the blue ox, are from Maine, U.S.A.
Paul said, "Maine's too small. I don't want to stay."

Some say that they live in Alaska these days.
It's way up north in the U.S.A.

There is so much room there. There is lots of space.
They can rumble and tumble. It is a great place.

That's where they are, Paul and his ox that is blue.
If you meet them someday, please ask, "How do you do?"

Tell what you know.

1. What color is the ox?
2. What do Babe and Paul Bunyon do?

Practice Page

Name the body parts. Cut. Paste. Make a puppet of Paul Bunyon.

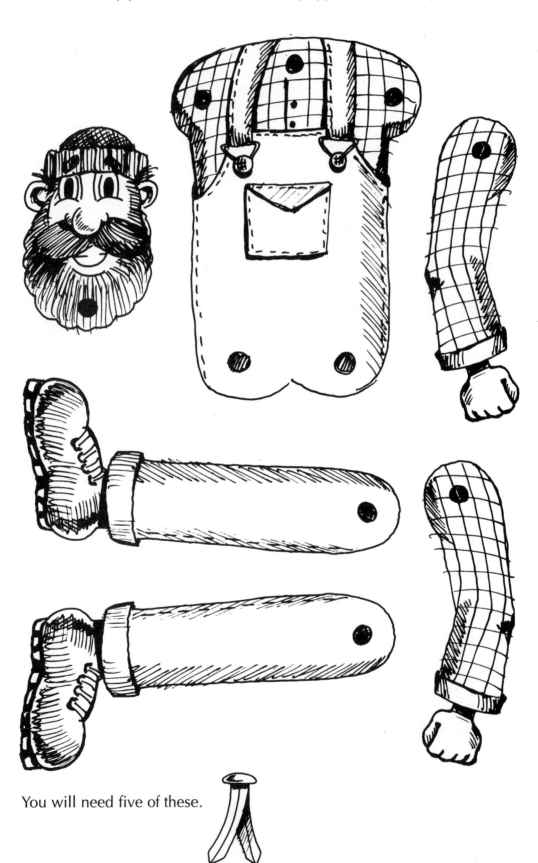

You will need five of these.

Ten Tales for Teaching English © Good Year Books.

Application Page

Can you find the place?

Paul and Babe used to live in Maine. Color it red.

Paul and Babe live in Alaska now. Color it orange.

Where do you live now? _____ Color it green.

Where are you from?

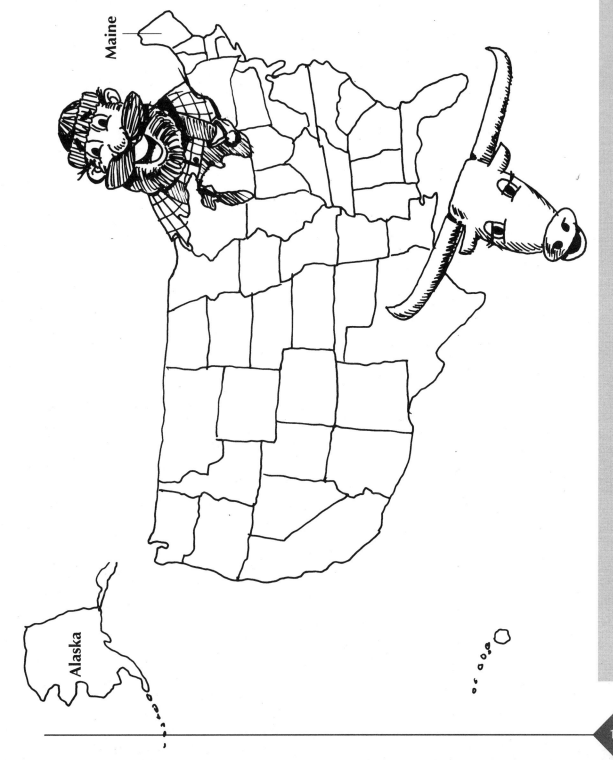

Evaluation Page

	Free Space	

Evaluation Page

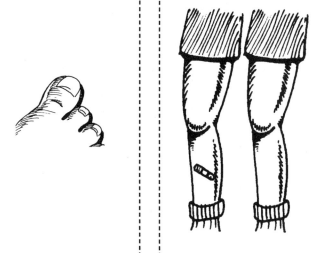

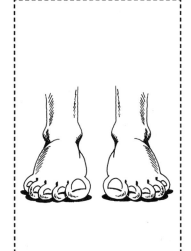

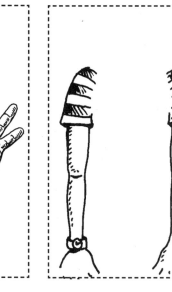

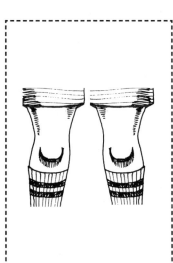

meat

fish

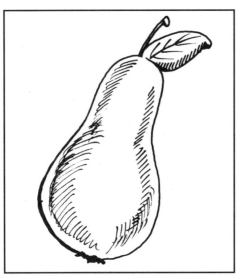

pear

plum

peach

eggs

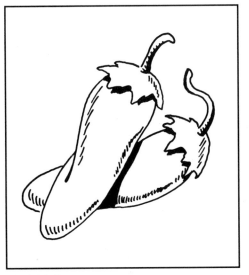

peppers

bun

flour

milk

carrots

potatoes

broccoli

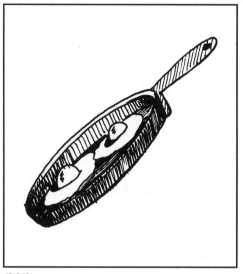

pan

bread

wheat

ant

cow

dog

rooster

horse

goat

ox

firefly

rabbit

wolf

bear

fox

hen

cat

duck

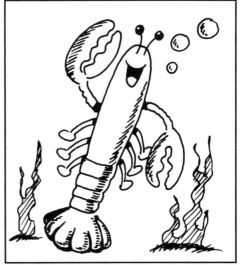

lobster

tiger

bears

king

fairy

Ten Tales for Teaching English © Good Year Books.

Flashcards

161

troll

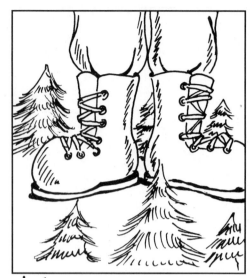

giant

farmer

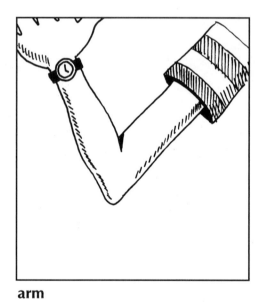

arm

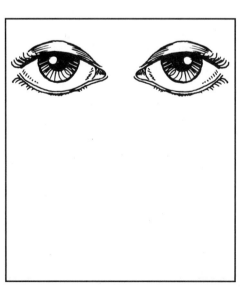

eyes

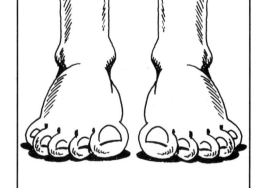

feet

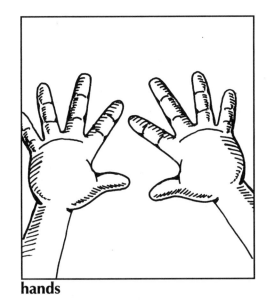

hands

head

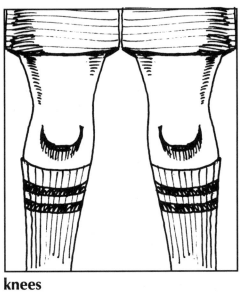

knees

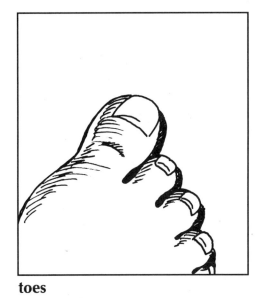

toes

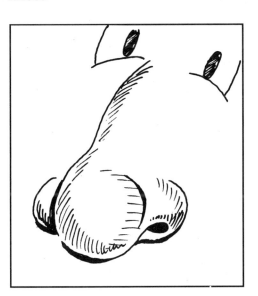

nose

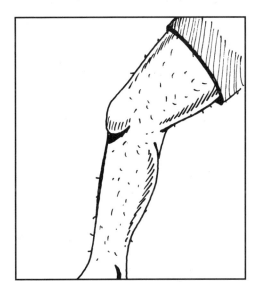

leg

tree

mountain

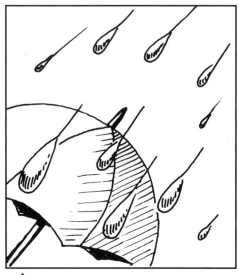

rain

sun

cloud

goats

Ten Tales for Teaching English © Good Year Books.

Make Your Own Flashcards

Ten Tales for Teaching English © Good Year Books.

Here are some flashcard games to use with the stories.

Look! Copy and cut out the flashcards for the new vocabulary for the story. Place them on the chalkboard ledge and review with children. Instruct children to close their eyes. Take one card away and then have them open their eyes. Say, "Look! What's missing?" Encourage students to use complete sentences when answering.

Matching Make two copies of the flashcards and cut them out. Review the vocabulary with children. Place the flashcards face down on a desk or table and have children take turns turning over two at a time. If the cards match, they get to keep them. Encourage students to say the new vocabulary words as they turn over the cards. The child with the most cards at the end of the game wins.

Card Game Make two copies of the flashcards and cut them out. Review the vocabulary with children. Deal an equal amount of cards to each player. Have children keep their cards hidden from their classmates. Have children take turns choosing a card from the player on their right. If they choose a card that matches one of theirs, they can put the pair on the table and name it. When a child runs out of cards, the game ends. The child with the most pairs at the end of the game wins.

Do You Have? Make two copies of the flashcards and cut them out. Review the vocabulary with children. Deal an equal amount of cards to each player. Have children keep their cards hidden from their classmates. Have children ask the player on their right if they have a specific card: "Do you have a bear?" If the player on the right has the card, he/she must give it to that child who then lays the pair on the table and names it. If the child doesn't have the card, he/she replies, "No, I don't." The turn goes to the next player. The player with the most pairs at the end of the game wins.

Where Is It? Place the flashcards in different spots in the classroom. Ask children, "Where is the (bear)?" The child who finds it first and identifies it correctly gets to keep the card. The child with the most cards at the end of the game wins. Children with more English background might tell where the flashcard is: "The bear is under the chair."

Flashcard Games

Bingo Give children an empty grid with nine spaces that will fit the flashcards. (See page 154). Give or have students make nine markers for the game. Give them copies of nine related flashcards, such as body parts, and have them paste them, in any order, in the grid. Play Bingo by randomly calling out the vocabulary words and having children place a marker on the picture as you say it. The child who gets three in a row, first, wins. To make the game more interesting, give children more than nine flashcards to choose from. The game can also be played so that one in each corner wins. This is called Corner Bingo.

Puppet Shows: Act It Out! Use the corresponding flashcards for each story. Give children copies of the characters and props, and have them either paste them on brown lunch bags or use sticks to create puppets. For children who are limited in English, read the story and have them act it out with the puppets they have created. You can also assign various children to be the characters and have them act out their parts as you read them. Children who are already reading and writing in English can read the various dialogue sections and act out the story as they are reading.

Felt Board Option Any activities or games that require placing flashcards or realia on the chalkboard ledge also work well with felt boards. Purchase a large felt board (2½ x 1½ feet) at a teacher's supply store or make one yourself. To use the flashcards with the felt board, glue 1½ inch squares of felt onto the back of the flashcards. There are many ways to use a felt board with students. You might cut out illustrations of the story characters and place them on the felt board as each is introduced. After you have read a story, students can refer to the felt board as they talk about the story or they can sequence the illustrations on the felt board to retell the story.

Ten Tales for Teaching English © Good Year Books.

Cole, Joanna. *Best Loved Folktales of the World*. New York: Doubleday, 1983.

———. *The Read-Aloud Treasury: Favorite Nursery Rhymes, Poems, Stories, and More for the Very Young*. New York: Doubleday, 1988.

McCarthy, Tara. *Multicultural Fables and Fairy Tales: Stories and Activities to Promote Literacy*. New York: Scholastic, 1993.

Offen, Hilda. *A Treasury of Bedtime Stories*. New York: Simon and Schuster, 1981.

Osborne, Mary Pope. *American Tall Tales*. New York: Alfred A. Knopf Books for Young Readers, 1991.

Philip, Neil. *The Illustrated Book of Fairy Tales*. New York: DK Publishing, 1997.

Sierra, Judy and Robert Kaminski. *Multicultural Folktales: Stories to Tell Young Children*. Phoenix, AZ: Oryx Press, 1991.

Sierra, Judy. *Nursery Tales Around the World*. New York: Houghton Mifflin Company, 1996.

Stern, Anita. *Tales from Many Lands: An Anthology of Multicultural Folk Literature*. Lincolnwood, IL: NTC/Contemporary Publishing Company, 1996.

Yolen, Jane. *Favorite Folktales from Around the World*. New York: Pantheon Books, 1988.